BS 538.3 .T43 2008
Thatcher, Adrian.
The savage text

D0988953

The Savage Text

Parkland College Library
2400 West Bradley Avenue
Champaign, IL 61821

Blackwell Manifestos

In this new series major critics make timely interventions to address important concepts and subjects, including topics as diverse as, for example: Culture, Race, Religion, History, Society, Geography, Literature, Literary Theory, Shakespeare, Cinema, and Modernism. Written accessibly and with verve and spirit, these books follow no uniform prescription but set out to engage and challenge the broadest range of readers, from undergraduates to postgraduates, university teachers, and general readers – all those, in short, interested in ongoing debates and controversies in the humanities and social sciences.

Already Published

Forthcoming

The Savage Text

The Use and Abuse of the Bible

Adrian Thatcher

WILEY-BLACKWELL

A John Wiley & Sons, Ltd., Publication

Parkland College Library
2400 West Bradley Avenue
Champaign, IL 61821

This edition first published 2008
© 2008 Adrian Thatcher

Blackwell Publishing was acquired by John Wiley & Sons in February 2007. Blackwell's publishing program has been merged with Wiley's global Scientific, Technical, and Medical business to form Wiley-Blackwell.

Registered Office
John Wiley & Sons Ltd, The Atrium, Southern Gate, Chichester, West Sussex, PO19 8SQ, United Kingdom

Editorial Offices
350 Main Street, Malden, MA 02148-5020, USA
9600 Garsington Road, Oxford, OX4 2DQ, UK
The Atrium, Southern Gate, Chichester, West Sussex, PO19 8SQ, UK

For details of our global editorial offices, for customer services, and for information about how to apply for permission to reuse the copyright material in this book please see our website at www.wiley.com/wiley-blackwell.

The right of Adrian Thatcher to be identified as the author of this work has been asserted in accordance with the Copyright, Designs and Patents Act 1988.

All rights reserved. No part of this publication may be reproduced, stored in a retrieval system, or transmitted, in any form or by any means, electronic, mechanical, photocopying, recording or otherwise, except as permitted by the UK Copyright, Designs and Patents Act 1988, without the prior permission of the publisher.

Wiley also publishes its books in a variety of electronic formats. Some content that appears in print may not be available in electronic books.

Designations used by companies to distinguish their products are often claimed as trademarks. All brand names and product names used in this book are trade names, service marks, trademarks or registered trademarks of their respective owners. The publisher is not associated with any product or vendor mentioned in this book. This publication is designed to provide accurate and authoritative information in regard to the subject matter covered. It is sold on the understanding that the publisher is not engaged in rendering professional services. If professional advice or other expert assistance is required, the services of a competent professional should be sought.

Library of Congress Cataloging-in-Publication Data

Thatcher, Adrian.
The savage text : the use and abuse of the Bible / Adrian Thatcher.
p. cm.—(Blackwell manifestos)
Includes bibliographical references and index.
ISBN 978-1-4051-7016-1 (pbk. : alk. paper)—ISBN 978-1-4051-7017-8 (hardcover : alk. paper)
1. Bible—Use. 2. Bible—Criticism, interpretation, etc. 3. Hate in the Bible. 4. Hate—Biblical teaching. 5. Hate—Religious aspects—Christianity. 6. Discrimination—Religious aspects—Christianity. I. Title.
BS538.3.T43 2008
220.608—dc22
2008004419

A catalogue record for this book is available from the British Library.

Set in 11.5/13.5pt Bembo
by SPi Publisher Services, Pondicherry, India
Printed in Singapore by Fabulous Printers Pte Ltd

1   2008

30.00

for
Caroline Major

Contents

Contents

Acknowledgments

This is a work that has been nearly 45 years in the making. In my first term at Regent's Park College, Oxford (1962), I heard lectures which offered escape from the fundamentalism which, as a teenager, had brought me the gift of faith, but presented it in a bubble of exclusivism, biblical literalism, and pseudo-certainty. Among the Baptists and Anglicans with whom I have made my spiritual home in the intervening years I have been dismayed at the growing influence of literal interpretations of the Bible which, despite their popularity among some sections of Christian people, frequently harms them, sacrifices the credibility of Christian faith among potential converts, and spreads damaging effects well beyond the churches. The savage use of the Bible in relation to sexual minorities in recent decades has galvanized me to suggest in this book a different way of receiving and proclaiming the words and works of God, of which the Bible speaks.

Acknowledgments along the way are too numerous to mention, so I shall confine them to the period covered by the writing of the book. I cherish the long discussions about the project with Michael Lawler in Omaha, Nebraska, and the strong encouragement he gave me. I thank Andrew Linzey (Oxford) for his positive and encouraging endorsement of the book at the proposal stage. I thank my colleagues at Exeter for sharing with me their interest, support, erudition, academic integrity, and friendship. They create an atmosphere where theological research and creativity thrive. In particular I thank

Acknowledgments

Francesca Stavrakopoulou for reading and commenting perspicuously on the chapters where I tangle with the Hebrew Bible, and Tim Gorringe who read the entire manuscript and gave me valuable advice. I thank Michael Northcott (Edinburgh) for reading large chunks of text on the apocalypse and giving me helpful guidance.

Once again I thank Caroline Major for her hawk-eyed proof-reading and indexing of my work. This is the sixth book on which we have worked together. She has been tireless in encouraging me through all of these projects. Caroline has a special place in my life. To her this work is dedicated.

A.T.

January 2008

Part I

What Is "The Savage Text"?

1

The "Savage Text"?

The Bible as an Idol?

The Bible has become Christianity's most acute problem. In some parts of the Christian Church the text of scripture rivals or even exceeds in importance the very reality of the God to whom the scripture points. This is a remarkable irony. The heirs to the movement that smashed countless icons, paintings, statues, and stained-glass windows on the grounds of one of the Ten Commandments ("You shall not make for yourself an idol in the form of anything in heaven above or on the earth beneath or in the waters below" – Exodus 20:4[1]), have installed an idol that exceeds them all.

One way of exposing the elevation of the Bible is to examine one of the names which has been attached to it, the "Word of God," or "God's Word." The Bible and the Church say God's Word is Jesus Christ. "The Word became flesh …" (John 1:14). The term "the Word" refers in John's Gospel to Jesus Christ. The Word is the divine self-communication. All Christians (as far as I know), including the growing number of **evangelical**, **conservative**, and **literalistic** ones, accept this belief unanimously. Of course they do – it's in the Bible! Jesus Christ is what God "speaks" to the whole creation. Christ is God's own self-disclosure. It is a core belief in all the churches. The problem is that some Christians combine this core belief with a further, non-core belief with which it is incompatible. The damaging add-on is the claim that *the Bible* is also the Word of God. But the

Bible does not make this claim. (How could it, for it has no consciousness of itself?) No, this is a modern **ideology** *about* the Bible and about which the Bible and the Creeds know nothing. It is a colossal mistake, and one which cannot be rectified or normalized by being constantly repeated.

Once the Bible is identified with the Word of God the text of scripture rivals or even replaces the Word of God, which is Jesus Christ. This is a disaster, for as St. Paul observed in a comparable context, "the letter kills, but the Spirit gives life" (2 Corinthians 3:6). **Biblicism** becomes **bibliolatry**, the actual *worship* of the Bible by assigning it the same status as that which is accorded by Christians to Jesus Christ. The Person is replaced by the proposition: flesh by words; the Word of God by written, and much-disputed, text. Speaking for **Anglicans** who are confronted with biblicism in many of their churches, Maggi Dawn wisely advises, "So while we owe it to ourselves and our tradition to guard and treasure a high view of the Bible, we need to avoid venerating scripture excessively, to the point where it displaces Christ the Word, and silences the capacity of Christ the Word to speak through the words on the page."[2]

This book is written in part to defend innocent Christian victims of this mistaken elevation of the Bible, for it has deleterious consequences for Christian ethics, for the personal conduct of millions of Christians all over the world, for the social and moral teaching of the churches, and, wherever it has influence, for politics. Christians all over the world are following the Bible instead of following Christ. But the main reason for writing *The Savage Text* is itself evangelical. The Church's mission is to spread the **good news** of Jesus Christ. This mission is frequently impaired by the ideological biblicism that accompanies it. This book makes a small contribution to the removal of this impairment.

The "savage text" is the name this book gives to the Bible (or passages from it) when its use results in the marginalization, or persecution, or victimization, of any of the people or creatures for whom (according to the Christian **Gospel**) Christ died. The savage text, it must be stressed, is not the Bible. It is not those parts of the Bible that depict or authorize violence. There is plenty of violence in the Bible, but the savage text does not refer straightforwardly to these passages. That there is much violence in the Bible is unsurprising since the biblical books were compiled over a period of some 700 years in the land, still war-torn, of Palestine, and the oldest parts probably date from the tenth century BCE, possibly slightly earlier. No, the savage text is not the Bible. It is what Christians have made of the Bible when they have used its pages to endorse cruelty, hatred, murder, oppression, and condemnation, often of other Christians. The savage text is what the Bible, or parts of it, becomes when it enables Christians to convert the good news of God's revealed love in Jesus Christ into the bad news that people are the wrong color, or race, or gender, or denomination, or orientation, or religion, or class, or empire, just because they differ from the Christians who are preaching this bad news. The savage text belongs to a "mind-set" that authorizes condemnation of any view or practice which is not that of its official or most powerful readers. When the Bible becomes a savage text, the theology that is proclaimed from it is already faulty. The savage text makes hatred holy. It makes seekers after truth its jealous guardians. Perhaps the worst feature of the savage text is the divine authority it claims for its strictures. The savage text is implicated in the moral case against Christianity. Who wants to defend a faith that customizes hatred?

The vision for this book dawned on me during my involvement over the last two decades in the bitter arguments within the churches about sexuality. Readers will know that the Christian churches are presently locked in damaging controversies over sexuality and gender, and in particular over homosexuality. Indeed the **Anglican Communion** of churches, to one of which I belong, is in danger of splitting itself apart over these questions. These controversies have resulted in the frequent misunderstanding, misrepresentation, and fear of sexual minorities, especially of homosexual people, inside and outside the churches. Such people are frequently victims of Christian **homophobia**. They suffer the pain of rejection that compulsory heterosexuality enforces upon them.

The Savage Text does not contribute directly to the resolution of these debilitating arguments. Rather, it asks how Christians have been able to conduct, in public and on a global scale, arguments that appear to have exposed prejudice, fear, and hatred to the extent that the very mission of the churches in the world has been compromised. Churches all over the world are arguing about these matters, and with regard to homosexuality (but not in other areas such as divorce and further marriage) it is probably fair to say that conservative views have prevailed. My interest was alerted to how conservative Christians have used the Bible in their assertions about lesbian and gay people, their relationships, and their place in the Church, the priesthood, and the **episcopate**. Gradually, and with increasing horror, I began to form the opinion that this use of scripture might resemble earlier uses of it, when Christians victimized children, women, Jews, the disabled, witches, people of color, slaves, scientists, criminals, heretics, and even animals, nature, and the environment. This kind of Bible use is intolerable and should have no place at all in Christianity, in any version of it. Neither is its misuse confined to fundamentalists or extremists who can be neatly differentiated from the more "mainstream" type of Christian view. Dozens of respectable bishops and their carefully chosen theological advisors lend their episcopal weight to savage, exclusionary policies which they claim to find in the Bible. I have concentrated mainly on manifestations of the savage text in Protestantism and Anglicanism, but there are also references throughout to Roman Catholic teaching. Since Protestant churches have no **Magisterium** or central teaching authority, and generally do not value tradition, the weight of interpretation that the Bible is required to bear is greater in these churches. The title, *The Savage Text*, began to suggest itself. It is the name I give to uses of the Bible which convert the good news the Bible brings to the world into *the savage text* that persecutes, condemns, and banishes. *The Savage Text* lays bare these savage interpretations of scripture, and shows that there is a "shadow side" to Christianity that remains disturbingly alive.

The Savage Text is neither a work of social science investigating religious behavior nor an attack on Christian faith by one of its opponents. It is a Christian theological work that is written for the sake of the future of Christianity. The Christian faith professes the self-giving love of God in Christ as the basis of its existence, mission, and practice. For it to be credible in its third millennium it must recover its vocation as the embodiment of the divine love, and its practice of the **Great Commandments** and the **Golden Rule**. It learns this vocation from the Bible. Thankfully in every generation including our own, there have been many faithful Christians who read the Bible in immensely fertile and creative ways, and who inspire the Church in fulfilling its vocation. Their presence in the Church is thankfully acknowledged here, but it is not the subject of the present work. For there is much in the Bible that, without due care, lends itself to work *against* this vocation. For the good of the Gospel it is time to devote attention to this, to examine how it works, and to seek to minimize its influence.

The readership of the book is likely to be of two kinds. Students of theology, religious studies, and ethics will find much here about the use and abuse of the Bible in relation to ethical questions, historical and contemporary. But since the Bible and its continuing use is of interest beyond the demands of the curriculum in universities and colleges (and since the *Manifesto* series is concerned with broad issues in the humanities and the social sciences), I hope to attract that mythical character beloved of publishers, the "general reader." Specifically, there are thousands of potential readers outside or on the fringes of the churches who remain interested in living, practical, intelligible theology. Some are puzzled by the obsession of churches with issues to do with sexuality; other readers may be curious about the religious roots of homophobia, and anxious to see the churches more obviously striving to be welcoming and inclusive communities. There are many members of churches who are weary of over-cautious or censorious leaderships, and who long for a more adventurous, less risk-averse way of "being church." There are millions of people who define themselves as "spiritual" yet think there is a moral deficiency within the churches at the present time. Since the harm caused by the savage text extends beyond the boundaries of the churches, there should be interest in it from beyond these boundaries also. In short, there are countless general readers, and I hope to attract some of these as well as students pursuing their university studies. It is with general readers in mind that a glossary has been included at the back of the book for all names and terms in bold type in the text, and why the names of biblical books are included in full (and not by standard abbreviations).

The Savage Text is unique in that it is a book about the Bible that allows itself to be molded by actual Bible use in and by the churches. I won't be trying too hard to expose **fundamentalism**. That has already been well done.[3] But a characteristic of fundamentalism is that it is impervious to criticism and indeed thrives upon it. I am more concerned with the inroads made by a conservative biblicism in many of the churches. It is 30 years since Dennis Nineham wrote *The Use and Abuse of the Bible*,[4] and 45 years since his *The Church's Use of the Bible, Past and Present*.[5] John Barton's admirable *People of the Book?*[6] is 20 years old, and concentrates on the *authority* of the Bible, whereas I already locate that old question in the separation of the Bible from other sources such as tradition, reason, and of course church. Keith Ward's excellent *What the Bible Really Teaches: A Challenge for Fundamentalists*[7] makes similar proposals to mine, except that I think "what the Bible really teaches" begs further questions (not least because Jehovah's Witnesses and others make similar claims), and that the Bible has to be understood more overtly through the faith of the Church which produced it. Ward does not concentrate on examples of *historical* Bible use as I am about to do. *The Savage Text* concentrates on the bizarre results that arise out of the excessive veneration of the Bible, and offers proposals for avoiding textual savagery in future.

The perspective taken in the book is both traditional and progressive. There is no truck here with a theological **liberalism** that reduces the contents of Christianity to the narrow scope of the "**enlightened**" Western mind, or that replaces the God of Jesus Christ and the Creeds of the Church with whatever anyone takes God to be, or that assumes all religions or even all versions of religions are equal before they have even been compared with one another. The book is *traditional* and conservative in locating itself in the tradition defined by the classic Creeds of the Church (none of which contains a doctrine of scripture or ideology of the Bible). The book is *progressive* in allying itself with the lively influences within Christian traditions that encourage change so that "the faith that was once for all entrusted to the saints" (Jude 3) is able to retain its freshness and seductive appeal. If to be "liberal" is to believe that "genuine faith is committed to the search for truth, wherever it comes from," that "God invites us to do our believing in ways appropriate to the twenty-first century," that "We never have absolute certainty," and that "Only God is infallible,"[8] then this work is unashamedly liberal too.

The tone and style of such a work represents a challenge. On the one hand there will be philosophical, theological, and historical argument which, if it is to be successful, must be sharp, forensic, and clinically efficient. On the other hand, there is little point in perpetuating the polemics that Christians hurl at each other. It must be possible to demolish poor arguments without demolishing the people who are taken in by them. There are deeper reasons why a peaceable tone is required. Anyone who argues, as I do, for a radically inclusive Christian Church, cannot, without scoring a spectacular own goal, alienate or exclude those Christians who already belong to it and with whom one presently disagrees. And anyone who disputes the claim of another to have privileged access to truth cannot simultaneously claim to have privileged access to truth either. In much of what I say I may be wrong. In the end one can only strive for clarity, offer arguments, and learn from people with whom one disagrees. This is important in any discipline, and vital in the Church. If there are lapses of charity in what follows, I apologize for these in advance.

The Manifesto of "The Savage Text"

Authors in the Blackwell *Manifesto* series can be expected to court controversy. They have a manifesto (an Italian term meaning "denunciation"), a *manifestus* or public written statement about which there may be little public agreement. It will not be easy to balance controversy with charity. This is my manifesto. I hold:

First, that there are two principal types of Bible use current among Christians. By "type" I mean "a number of things or persons sharing a particular characteristic, or set of characteristics, that causes them to be regarded as a group."[9] There are as many kinds of Bible-reading as there are readers, but the set of characteristics that reduces to two main groups concerns what the Bible is *for*. The first type assumes that God has made Godself known to humanity through the human being, Jesus Christ. The Bible *witnesses* to the truth of God revealed in Jesus. Everyone can know God through Jesus, and the Bible has been, and remains, the indispensable witness to the divine self-disclosure that was Christ. This might well be called "the witness principle." The most famous Protestant theologian of the twentieth century, Karl Barth, made a succinct statement of the witness principle:

> The Word of God is God Himself in Holy Scripture. For God once spoke as Lord to Moses and the prophets, to the Evangelists and apostles. And now through their written word He speaks as the same Lord to His Church. Scripture is holy and the Word of God, because by the Holy Spirit it became and will become to the Church *a witness to divine revelation*.[10]

The second type of Bible use, in practice if not always overtly in theory, assumes that God has made Godself known to humanity equally through the human being, Jesus Christ, *and* in scripture. In this second type, the Bible does not merely witness to the truth of God revealed in Jesus. It shares the truth of God which is Jesus. Jesus *and* the Bible *together* constitute God's truth. On this view the Bible becomes, or is in constant danger of becoming, a co-equal source of God's revelation. The Bible on this view is not unfairly regarded as an inspired guidebook to supernatural realities and earthly ethical practices. The Word of God is God's self-communication to humanity. That self-communication is supremely Jesus Christ, but not of course confined exclusively to him. God can "speak" in countless ways to people. Reading the Bible for millions of Christians has been and remains one such way. But, as we shall shortly see, the text of the Bible is also incriminated in countless atrocities and acts of cruelty. Problems arise within the "guidebook view" when all scripture is regarded "in equal measure as the Word of God."[11] Still worse problems arise when the text of scripture is assumed to *be* the Word of God, when it is clearly and offensively inconsistent with the divine Love revealed in Jesus Christ. If the Bible is to be called "the Word of God" (as Barth does), then it is in a derivative and secondary sense that is "a witness to divine revelation." I think it is misleading to ascribe that name to the Bible.

Second, that the first type, or "witness principle," is the historical, classical, and even **Reformed** way of handling scripture. Fundamentalist and many evangelical Christians adhere to the second, mistaken, view. But many other Christians also affirm the second view, not because they belong to any particular party in the Church, but out of an excessive reverence for scripture, often as a result of neglect of other sources of God's self-communication such as tradition, reason, wisdom, experience, nature, art, beauty, and so on.

Third, that whenever the guidebook view is held equally with the witness view or even preferred to it, the revelation of God in Christ is endangered, compromised, or even denied. Divine authority can then be claimed for all kinds of horrors such as slavery, the persecution of Jews and other races, the beating of children, the burning of witches, male gender superiority, compulsory heterosexuality, and so on. The Bible in these cases ceases to be holy because it ceases to witness to God's Word in Christ, and becomes instead a savage text. It follows,

Fourth, that whenever the savage text is proclaimed, it undermines Christian faith in the Word of God made flesh, and causes suffering, injustice, and endless division among Christians (because the Bible inevitably means different things to them).

Fifth, that the popularity among many Christians of the savage text is gained by offering a bogus *simplicity*, a guidebook to dissipate the complex realities of late modern life. The savage text also offers a *bogus*

identity, continually reinforced by defining all those with whom its readers disagree (just about everyone in the end) as wrong. Opponents are simply Other.

Sixth, that the designation "People of the Book" can never be applied to Christians without converting Christianity into a faith more like some of its rivals, thereby negating its profound distinctiveness as the people of the God who, in order to reach God's people, became one of them. By some dizzying irony, the dominant attitude to the Bible among many conservative Christians resembles more the dominant Islamic attitude to the Qur'an than an authentic witness to Jesus Christ.

And *seventh*, that, in the name of the One to whom the Bible bears its essential witness, Christians must renounce overt and covert bibliolatry.

The Argument of the Book

This, then, is the manifesto. Chapter 2 considers the possibility that the Bible has been used as a savage text in the bitter current arguments about sexuality among the churches. That possibility raises the further question whether the condemnation of "homosexual practice" is an extension of an older savage use of the Bible against other minorities which exhibit difference. That question is the subject of part II.

Chapter 2 examines some examples of Bible use in support of the attempt to show that God disapproves of homosexuality. The failure to establish the conservative case, and the suffering that results from it, set the agenda for the rest of the book. Are there similarities between the repressive use of the Bible against sexual minorities and the repressive use of the Bible against many others?

Chapters 3–6 develop links between Bible use in present controversies over sexuality, and Bible use in other historical controversies. They will show how at other times the Bible became, or becomes, a savage text legitimizing the Christian mistreatment of people of color, slaves, non-Christians, the environment, children, Jews, women, and other minorities. It will show that a literal reading of particular passages of scripture, along with many other social, intellectual, and cultural factors, contributed to disgraceful practices and continues to do so.

In the aftermath of the damage that the undifferentiated appeal to scripture continues to do in converting it into a savage text, chapter 7 asks why this counter-Christian tradition at the heart of Christianity continues to hold sway. The pursuit of an answer leads to the uncovering of defects in the Protestant **Scripture Principle** and to the quest for a more charitable and Christ-like way of handling non-biblical books and nonconforming Christians. Chapter 8 disowns the epithet "People of the Book" as applicable to Christianity. Christian faith is faith in the **triune** God, made flesh in God the Word, to whom the Bible *and* tradition bear fallible witness. The tendency to "personalize" the Bible, and thereby to treat it as an object of devotion, is strenuously resisted. Some principles for the *peaceable* reading of the Bible are suggested. When the love of scripture replaces the love of God, the savage text reappears. The Christian scriptures are the compilation of the Christian Church which is still learning how to become a godly "community of readers," capable of honoring the self-giving God who is Love and whose Spirit leads into all truth.

There is a bewilderingly large and ever-growing number of English Bible translations, each favored by particular groups of readers. Which one should be used in this book? I have decided to use the King James or Authorized Version of 1611! Any deviation from this version was frowned upon in the Baptist Church where I first came to faith in 1959, but that is not the reason for using it here. The King James Version has had more influence in English-speaking countries, and over a much longer period, than all the other available English translations put together. I dusted off my well-worn and marked-up copy when writing this book for three reasons. First, it conveys a sense of historical weight. For nearly 350 years Protestant and Anglican Christians used this version and no other, and when newer translations began to appear (e.g., the Revised Version, in 1881) they were revisions of, not replacements for, this historical text. Second, it conveys a magisterial sense and an authoritative tone that no other English version has managed to achieve. In a sense that is hard to grasp today, many of the millions of Protestant Christians who used the Authorized Version believed that the inspiration of the Holy Spirit, who inspired the original manuscripts, extended also to the translators and compilers of this sacred work. Much of it they knew by heart, as well as by rote. And third, the renewed encounter with its archaic prose helps us to regain a sense of historical development, as well as the historical relativity of all attempts to convey the meanings of the ancient Hebrew and Greek texts. Whenever the unfamiliarity (or inaccuracy) of the Authorized Version becomes an obstacle, alternative readings are provided.

2

"Vile Affections": The Bible and Homosexuality

This chapter analyzes some recent examples of the use of the Bible in present controversies within the churches over the presence and practices of out gay and lesbian people. Second, it indicates the danger involved in using the Bible as a guidebook to acceptable behavior. Third, it examines the claim that same-sex love contradicts the created order described in Genesis 1. Finally the question is posed whether the biblical maneuvers that have been uncovered make better sense if they are understood to extend a long line of historical **exegesis** that has had catastrophic consequences for various minorities. That question gives rise to an examination in part II of the book, of comparable catastrophes.

Morality or Ideology?

In England and Wales consensual sex between men was partially decriminalized in 1967. Homosexuality was not removed from the register of psychological illnesses of the American Psychological Association until 1973. It is not surprising, then, that among an older generation the association between homosexuality and criminality remains. In the interests of charity it is necessary to point out that all of us inherit socio-cultural constraints, almost all of which are sanctioned to some degree by religion. Homosexual law reform is a step too far for millions of Christians with long memories, a legacy of Bible-based hostility to homosexual practice, and a natural dislike of being dubbed "homophobes" by their opponents. They are not responsible for this legacy, although they are seriously responsible for examining (or failing to examine) it. The Bible passage that is thought to forbid homosexual practice most clearly is in Romans:

> For this cause God gave them up unto vile affections: for even their women did change the natural use into that which is against nature: And likewise also the men, leaving the natural use of the woman, burned in their lust one toward another; men with men working that which is unseemly, and receiving in themselves that recompense of their error which was meet. (Romans 1:26–7)

According to a standard interpretation of these verses, sex between women and women and between men and men requires surrender to "vile affections," (*pathē atimias*) or as more modern translations put it, "shameful lusts,"[1] or "degrading passions."[2] It is contrary either to our natures as heterosexual persons, or to nature itself. It is the only passage in the Bible to mention lesbian sex directly, but it does so in explicit terms. Sexual acts between persons of the same sex are sinful. They inevitably lead to depravity and moral dissolution. In order to avoid grievous sin, homosexual people must remain celibate. (According to one version of this story, AIDS, a disease transmitted initially by gay men, is itself a punishment, and now millions of straight people suffer a similar punishment for promiscuity.) On the basis of this passage alone, the Bible clearly teaches that homosexuality is wrong. Other biblical passages confirm it. There is "a clear consistency within the Scriptures themselves on the moral issue of homosexual behavior." They are confirmed by "the Spirit of Truth whose Word they are," and by the Church's "living Tradition."[3] Registered same-sex partnerships or "gay marriages" must be opposed because they contradict the will of God, the Word of God, and the moral and natural law (both of which are created by God).

16

That is a possible interpretation. Here is another. The passage is not about homosexuality as we know it today. In any case, *all* passion is dishonorable in the New Testament: all affections vile.[4] Paul does not allow sexual desire in marriage either.[5] There is nothing especially disreputable about homosexual passion. Neither is there anything especially disreputable about the "unseemly" or "shameful" work that men get up to with men. The word used here for "shameful" applies in other biblical contexts to the shame associated with sexual organs, or to feces (Deuteronomy 23:14–15).[6] The sexual organs are shameful in Jewish culture, but they are not sinful, any more than producing feces is. Since we don't know what Paul means by "nature" we shouldn't conclude that lesbian sex is contrary to it. Indeed when Paul uses that phrase (*para phusin*) a second time in the same letter, he uses it in connection with the work of God grafting the Gentiles into the olive tree that represents the Jews (Romans 11:24).[7] That wasn't sinful – it was a work of sheer grace. In any case we don't know that Paul had in mind women having sex with women. Because he refers to the women as "their women" we know he refers to their belonging to men (as every woman did in the ancient world). Perhaps they were having sex with other men than the ones who owned them? That would also be against nature or at least against the natural order. Perhaps these women were having non-coital sex with men: that too might pass as against nature.[8] If so, the solitary reference to lesbianism in the Bible disappears. Male homosexual desire is *not* a sin in these verses. "Fornication" is included in the list of sins mentioned in Romans 1:29–32, but not homosexuality. "The sexual practices of the Gentiles are, then, not a sin, a crime against God to be punished; they are themselves the 'recompense' inflicted on the Gentiles for their deliberate turning away from the truth."[9] If Robin Scroggs is right in claiming that in the ancient world the only form of homosexual activity that was openly discussed was pederasty,[10] no Christian alive disagrees with Paul's repudiation of it. Since the New Testament does not deal with contemporary cases where people of the same sex makes lifelong vows of commitment to each other based on their love for one another, it is disingenuous to use this scripture or any other to proscribe same-sex marriages and civil partnerships.[11]

17

There are at least two more reasons for thinking the standard interpretation cannot hold, both of them to do with the overall argument Paul makes in Romans 1:18–32. He writes to Christians in Rome who, prior to their conversion, were Jews, and so were very familiar with the Jewish scriptures which are preserved in the Christian Bible. In his opening section he recounts how Jews have generally regarded Gentiles or non-Jews. As a Jew himself he would not have found this difficult. Fifteen verses are devoted to a description of the perverse condition which arises from their rejection of the God of Israel. The sting in the argument lies in its tail, for it deflates the arrogant view that, while Gentiles stand condemned for their sins, Jews do not. Paul is quite clear that *it is wrong for Christians to condemn the Gentiles for any of their sins*:

> Therefore thou art inexcusable, O man, whosoever thou art that judgest: for wherein thou judgest another, thou condemnest thyself; for thou that judgest doest the same things ... And thinkest thou this, O man, that judgest them which do such things, and doest the same, that thou shalt escape the judgment of God? (Romans 2:1, 3)

The very verses that are intended to preclude the condemnation of the sins of Gentiles are turned by the modern moralists into a justification for doing precisely what the argument of the text forbids. For in judging others, as Jesus also said (Matthew 7:1–2), we judge ourselves. As Paul would have it, it was necessary for these Roman Christians to abandon their smug judgments about Gentiles, for the moral superiority associated with it was actually harming their souls. In Paul's thought, everyone (Jews and Gentiles or "Greeks") has "sinned, and come short of the glory of God." (Romans 3:23) Getting right with God, he thought, was no longer a matter of keeping the law or avoiding the sins that the Gentiles committed. For Paul it was a matter of accepting in faith what God had done for all humankind through the death and resurrection of Jesus Christ. What irony that

18

the principal passage of scripture normally used to condemn same-sex relations is also a principal passage forbidding the condemnation of anyone, by anyone, for any reason!

The second reason for doubting the traditional interpretation of these verses is that Christians, or at least those who are historically minded, do not accept the premises of Paul's argument, so the conclusions will be rejected too. Paul thinks that before Christ the Gentiles were well capable of recognizing and worshiping the one true God (Romans 1:19–23). By their actions they rejected God. Forsaking Hebrew monotheism they became Gentile polytheists, making images "like to corruptible man, and to birds, and fourfooted beasts, and creeping things" (Romans 1:23). But historians of religion agree that monotheism did not come first, and that Jews were not immune from polytheism themselves. "In sum, modern people, even Christians, do not believe the mythological structure that provides the logic for Paul's statements about homosexuality in Romans 1."[12]

The simple point to be carried forward from this discussion of Romans 1 is that what Paul meant then, and the implications for us now of what he might have meant, are and are likely to remain undecided. It follows that if all homosexual activity is wrong, the case for its wrongness is nothing like as strong as its advocates suggest. We have not even begun to consider how the concept of a sexual "orientation," and how the progress made in the scientific understanding of some forms of homosexuality, might obviate these negative judgments, even if apparently objective textual scholarship could successfully defend them. The same dilemmas attend the second apparent proof-text against homosexuality in Paul's writings, a warning that "neither fornicators, nor idolaters, nor adulterers, nor *effeminate, or abusers of themselves with mankind* ... shall inherit the kingdom of God" (1 Corinthians 6:9–10[13]). Immediately the problem of translating two Greek terms (*malakoi* and *arsenokoitai*) arises. An Anglican document affirms that "These have traditionally been seen as practising homosexuals, and understanding the text in this way has led to its being seen as clearly condemning homosexual behaviour as contrary to the law of God and as a bar to inheriting God's kingdom."[14] The document then goes on to examine dissenting interpretations before affirming "it is still the case that the consensus of scholarly opinion supports the traditional interpretation of these New Testament texts."[15] Really?

It is agreed that the common (and masculine) word *malakos* means "soft," so "the soft" are "the effeminate," a characteristic despised in the ancient world among men who were supposed to be in control, commanding, and firm, never displaying feminine qualities. The text is about men, not about all "practising" homosexuals. A promising way of understanding the rarer word *arsenokoitai* is to examine its use in other ancient contexts where it has to do with "some kind of economic exploitation, probably by sexual means: rape or sex by economic coercion, prostitution, pimping, or something of the sort."[16] Paul may have been denouncing paying for sex with rent boys, or "denouncing one very specific form of male–male sexual relationship which is part of the feminized way of life of one of the partners."[17] "Practising homosexuals" is a disingenuous term. Compare it with "practising *hetero*sexuals." Having sex with prostitutes is something "practising *hetero*sexuals" do. So is love-making within marriage. Is the latter to be condemned because of the existence of the former? Clearly not. "Practising" heterosexuals can enjoy matrimonial bliss and orgiastic debauchery. Practising homosexuals are doubtless capable of similar extremes. The slide from "some" to "all" is a casual logical mistake with colossal pastoral repercussions. So is the scholarly consensus wrong then? Very likely. Who knows? It is clear, though, that the objective meanings that scholars claim to find in their confident investigations are elusive – "oppressive ideologies have always in the modern world masqueraded as objective descriptions of 'the way things are.'"[18] We shall need to consider carefully the possibility, not that contemporary supporters of the traditional view are necessarily "homophobic," but whether "their writings about homosexuality participate in a cultural homophobia … that pervades much of modern Western culture." Should not Christians who use the Bible in this way consider whether they are transgressing one of the Ten Commandments, namely, "Thou shalt not bear false witness against thy neighbour" (Exodus 20:16; Deuteronomy 5:20)?

Another text used to condemn homosexual "practice" is the grand narrative in Genesis from which the term "sodomy" is derived. One evening a pair of angels visits the town of Sodom. Lot, Abraham's cousin and a legal immigrant to the town, mindful of his duties of hospitality towards these supernatural beings, gives them food and a bed for the night. But:

> before they lay down, the men of the city, even the men of Sodom, compassed the house round, both old and young, all the people from every quarter: And they called unto Lot, and said unto him, Where are the men which came in to thee this night? bring them out unto us, that we may know them. And Lot went out at the door unto them, and shut the door after him, And said, I pray you, brethren, do not so wickedly. Behold now, I have two daughters which have not known man; let me, I pray you, bring them out unto you, and do ye to them as is good in your eyes: only unto these men do nothing; for therefore came they under the shadow of my roof. (Genesis 19:4–8)

Our sense of the holiness of scripture should not inhibit the asking of hard moral questions about it. Bluntly here is a father who, in order to protect a couple of supernatural visitors from gang-rape, is prepared to hand over his daughters to be gang-raped instead. Nowhere in the narrative are this hasty proposal or his authority to make it criticized. (As we shall see in chapter 5, it is one of scores of texts where children do not exactly fare well in the scriptures.) Surely a story which casually records a father's betrayal of his daughters to a testosterone-crazed and murderous rabble cannot be used with much conviction by readers claiming high moral ground over same-sex relations? (Lot later in the chapter has sex with both his daughters. It is of course their fault for seducing him [Genesis 19:30–8]).

The critical study of these texts actually deflects much of the moral criticism of them. They are stories, and combinations of stories, and they are capable of making various points, in the case of Sodom about

21

the perils of neglecting the law governing the offering of hospitality to strangers ("thou shalt not oppress a stranger: for ye know the heart of a stranger, seeing ye were strangers in the land of Egypt" [Exodus 23:9]). That is certainly how Jesus understood the story (Matthew 10:15). Critical study finds **aetiological** explanations present in the stories. The geological presence of a pillar of salt on the landscape is "explained" by Lot's wife looking back as the city was destroyed (Genesis 19:26): the offspring of his incestuous coupling with his daughters become heads of tribes opposed to Israel (19:37–8) thereby "explaining" their ethnic inferiority, and so on.

It should not even be necessary to mention the injunction in the Old Testament "And if a man also lie with mankind, as he lieth with a woman, both of them have committed an abomination: they shall surely be put to death; their blood shall be upon them" (Leviticus 20:13 [and 18:22]). Yet the Roman Catholic Church uses the Sodom narrative and these injunctions in a typically savage way: "the deterioration due to sin continues in the story of the men of Sodom. There can be no doubt of the moral judgement made there against homosexual relations. In Leviticus 18:22 and 20:13, in the course of describing the conditions necessary for belonging to the Chosen People, the author excludes from the People of God those who behave in a homosexual fashion."[19] Surely if this injunction is to be obeyed, all 613 injunctions in the Old Testament are equally binding? Shellfish, and much else, "shall be an abomination unto you" (Leviticus 11:12). Which abominations are still abominable now, and which not? Perhaps the Vatican would prefer to have gays *killed*, as this text expressly requires? That is precisely what it did to 150 "Sodomites" in Spain (between 1570 and 1630), and many more at other times and in other places. Just to make plain the Inquisition's disapproval, the Spanish Sodomites were burned alive "without benefit of strangulation."[20]

There is in the Bible much condemnation of promiscuity of all kinds, and for good reasons. The late and disputed letter of Jude in the New Testament condemns promiscuous sexual relations between straight and same-sex people, and does so on the basis of the Sodom story. Here the theological grounds for condemning promiscuity are even stranger. There are randy angels who fancy earthly women. These "sons of God saw the daughters of men that they were fair; and they took them wives of all which they chose" (Genesis 6:2). They give birth to a race of giants, and "it repented the LORD that he had made man on the earth, and it grieved him at his heart" (6:6). According to the writer of Jude the sin of the randy angels was that they "kept not their first estate" (6), that is, they did not respect the social order which placed them above men and women. The angels went "after strange flesh" (7). That too constitutes the wrongness of same-sex relations. They are strange and contradict the patriarchal order.

Thoughtful Christians, gay or straight, are frankly embarrassed when their brothers[21] in Christ mount arguments like these which marginalize and discriminate against lesbian and gay people. Is it not truly astonishing that political, moral, and religious censure can be brought to bear on sexual minorities on the basis of such "evidence"? We do not inhabit the thought world where angels drop in for dinner, or get hassled by gangs of predatory men, or eye up nubile earthly women and have sex with them. Women sexually attractive to men have more trouble deflecting the male gaze and the predatory practices of earthlings than with staving off angels. Staving off randy angels was the New Testament argument for wearing the veil (1 Corinthians 11:10). No, same-sex couples enjoying the "strange flesh" of their partners will not conceive giants. One suspects that the ancient thought world was actually much richer in imagination, comprehension of human frailty and complexity, and possibly in expression, than the thought world of many contemporary Christians who have recourse to these strange narratives in order to maintain their fragile grip on compulsory heterosexuality. Already the case is building that the Bible is not being used in these arguments to proclaim good news, but rather to enforce the waning patriarchal and heterosexual order which seems incapable of self-scrutiny. It is being used as a savage text.

A Guidebook for Sexual Behavior?

A recent official statement of the churches of the Anglican Communion about homosexuality is the 1998 Lambeth Conference resolution 1.10. More fireworks can be expected when 850 bishops reassemble in 2008, discuss the same things, and reach similar conclusions.[22] The resolution "recognises that there are among us persons who experience themselves as having a homosexual orientation."[23] In the official Anglican mind, there are two types of homosexual in the Anglican Communion. The first type is celibate, and is commended for "seeking the pastoral care, moral direction of the Church, and God's transforming power for the living of their lives and the ordering of relationships." The second type comprises all the others, who need to be warned that the Church, "*in view of the teaching of Scripture*, upholds faithfulness in marriage between a man and a woman in lifelong union, and believes that abstinence is right for those who are not called to marriage."[24]

Well, the churches of the Anglican Communion also uphold the right to divorce for men and women in lifelong unions, almost whenever it suits, and their subsequent "further marriage,"[25] even though these practices are clearly against "the teaching of scripture," and, more crucially, *against the straightforward teaching of Jesus Christ himself.* Is that not an odd, selective, and discriminatory use of scripture, to say the least? So much, then, for "the teaching of scripture" being even-handedly applied. The Church rejects "homosexual practice as *incompatible with Scripture*," and "... calls on all our people to minister pastorally and sensitively to all irrespective of sexual orientation."[26] Not only is the resolution highly reactionary, it rejects and condemns the "irrational fear of homosexuals," without considering that irrational Christian teaching about homosexuality is largely responsible for precisely this outcome. It "cannot advise the legitimising or blessing of same sex unions nor ordaining those involved in same gender unions." Scripture, then, is at the root of all this. Not God. Not Christ. But the savage text.

There is a disdainful and unworthy double game of pretense going on here. Anglican bishops are pretending, for the sake of appeasing strident, reactionary Christian voices, that their bishops and clergy can "minister pastorally and sensitively" to lesbian and gay couples, while telling them that they can't be intimate with each other, because Scripture says so. And they are pretending that they are not responsible for the obvious link between their negative teaching about homosexuality and the "irrational fear of homosexuals" which continues to blight the lives of so many lesbian and gay people. Two nasty features of Protestant Christianity have now returned to haunt it in the present: the first is the over-reliance on the Bible that is a consequence of the rejection of much of the Catholic liturgical, devotional, and mystical theology and practice at the time of the Reformation. The Bible replaces so much else that its enhanced position comes to license the further neglect of reason, of tradition, and of experience. The second is an extensive discomfort regarding anything to do with sexuality and the body.

Witness or Guide?

It was claimed above that many Christians are as devoted to the Bible as they are to the One to whom the Bible bears witness. These Christians are not only fundamentalists and evangelicals. They are bishops, church leaders, and writers of sexuality reports. Once the Bible is elevated to the status of the Word of God, a status which the Bible itself reserves for Jesus Christ, the slide into dogmatism is almost certain to occur. A recent, fine example of an official document which demonstrates these perils is the Church of England House of Bishops' *Some Issues in Human Sexuality: A Guide to the Debate*. Mindful of what has already been said (see chapter 1 above) about the "guidebook view" of the Bible, I shall use it as a fine (and unwitting) example of this view.[27] The *Guide* sets out two incompatible views of the Bible, both of which it advocates.[28] On the one hand, Christians generally are said to see the Bible "as providing normative guidance for their sexual conduct."[29] On the other hand, Christians are said to see the Bible this way, very properly, because of the status they give "to the Bible as a whole as pointing to Christ, through whom God has revealed to his people what he is like, what he has done for them, and how they should respond to him."[30] Since this view of the Bible points away from itself to the person and work of Christ, it can be identified with "the witness view" of the Bible (which we also met earlier). The bishops adopt these designations explicitly. As they explain, Christians should read the Bible

> as a *witness* to the grace of God through which salvation is offered to us in fulfilment of God's covenant promises, and as *guide* to the path of Christian discipleship by which we may live appropriately in response to that grace. In terms of the specific issue of human sexuality it means reading the Bible in such a way as to discover how God's will for human sexual conduct gives expression to his grace, and what it means to respond rightly to him in this area of our lives.[31]

Later in the chapter these views are formally separated. The first view regards the Bible as "a guide to Christian discipleship." The second regards it "as a witness to the grace of God."[32] Throughout the rest of the document the first view prevails.

A primary source of confusion in the *Guide* and in the churches is the conflation of these two distinct views. Since the Bible points to Christ, it is clearly right to speak of it as a "witness" to him. Because Jesus is God, Jesus is God's revelation, and the Bible, like John the Baptist, is a witness to that. But when the Bible is thought to provide "normative guidance" for the conduct of Christians, it may then cease to be the witness to God's revelation, and *become* the revelation instead. The attempt to combine these views cannot succeed. One might expose the mistake by asking what a witness does. A witness sees or hears something, perhaps a crime, and testifies to others what she or he has seen or heard. But a witness to a crime is not the criminal! Yet this guidebook view makes an identification that is as crass as that. The witness must be detached from what is witnessed, and able to provide impartial evidence. John the Baptist was a witness to Jesus (though hardly an impartial one!) (John 1:6–8; 15).

The *Guide* is right to emphasize the status of the Bible as a witness to Christ. But the guidebook view is incompatible with it because it endorses the supposition that Christians should follow the Bible, instead of following the One to whom the Bible is a witness. If we already have a guidebook to tell us how to handle our sex lives, why do we need Jesus Christ as well? Is God in Christ our guide, or is the Bible our guide? It is a serious matter to confuse a witness to the truth with the One who is the Truth (John 14:6). John the Baptist was mistakenly confused with the Messiah, a rival, in fact, to Jesus himself (e.g., Matthew 11:1–19). The Gospel writers all needed to put clear, deep water between Jesus and John. And the Church of the present needs to put a similar distance between the One who reveals God and the writings that witness to that unrepeatable and unsurpassable revelation. This distinction between witness and guide, commendably introduced by the bishops, is crucially important. But the combination of them is a bad blunder from which their theological consultants should have spared them. The distinction requires choice, not synthesis.

The Bible, then, causes trouble for lesbians and gays, just as it did for Jews, heretics, slaves, people of color, and countless others in the lengthening roll call of persecuted minorities, all in the name of Christ. The Catechism of the Catholic Church teaches that "*Basing itself on Sacred Scripture,* which presents homosexual acts as acts of grave depravity, Tradition has always declared that 'homosexual acts are intrinsically disordered.'"[33] Once again, the savage text can be conveniently blamed for the persecution and calumniation of a minority. According to Southern Baptists of the USA the Bible condemns homosexuality as a sin,[34] and since the Bible "has God for its author, salvation for its end, and truth, without any mixture of error, for its matter,"[35] it cannot be comfortable to be a gay or lesbian Southern Baptist. Now there is a new late twentieth-century argument which finds in the Bible something called the "complementarity" of the sexes. Before we leave the Anglican bishops, we need to examine another theological line of persecution which has lodged itself in contemporary Catholic and Protestant thought.

A Man Needs a Woman?

> So God created man in his own image, in the image of God created he him; male and female created he them. And God blessed them, and God said unto them, Be fruitful, and multiply, and replenish the earth, and subdue it: and have dominion ... (Genesis 1:27–8)
>
> Therefore shall a man leave his father and his mother, and shall cleave unto his wife: and they shall be one flesh. (Genesis 2:24)

According to the *Guide* the New Testament is said to point us "back to the creation narratives ... as providing the proper framework for understanding what it means for us to be male and female before God and to relate together as such." God made us as men and women so we could have children and so we should not exist in solitude.[36]

> if we follow the Genesis narrative, we find that it depicts full sexual intercourse as taking place within a permanent and exclusive bond between two people of the opposite sex.
> The Genesis account of the creation of Eve from Adam focuses on two aspects of the relationship between them. The first is their complementarity and the second is their union.[37]

The interpretation that follows invites incredulity. Having tried to establish that these texts have "fixed meanings," the guidebook view of the Bible is now put to work, and Genesis 1 and 2 are required to bear a severe weight of interpretation.[38] These texts are thought to provide a timeless framework which regulates human sexuality and gender and which is authorized by God just because it appears in these texts.

The bishops understand that the use of these verses in the *New* Testament is decisive for Christians. Their argument seems to be: (1) the New Testament uses these narratives in a particular way. Therefore (2) we must use these narratives in the particular way that the New Testament does. But these premises are greatly overstated. Jesus refers to Genesis 1 and 2 in the context of criticizing the excessive practice of husbands divorcing wives (Matthew 19:3–9). The New Testament does not say the Old Testament gives us a theory of sexuality which it affirms. The New Testament interprets the Hebrew scriptures as pointing forward to the coming of the Messiah, Jesus Christ. To say Genesis provides a "framework for understanding what it means for us to be male and female before God" is already to offer interpretation well beyond what the text itself is able to authorize. The bishops are able to derive fixed meanings for "what it means" to be male and female, and just from this text! This is a classic example of biblical interpretation that attracts just criticism, viz., that passages of scripture have single, fixed meanings, and experts, either godly or academic or episcopal, can tell us what those privileged yet elusive meanings are.

If Genesis 1 and 2 miraculously provide us with such a framework, we cannot innocently bracket out that we now live at a time when 500 years of science and nearly 200 years of biblical criticism have hugely expanded our understanding both of the various subjects trea-ted in the creation narratives and of the narratives themselves. They have required "revisionism" of all of us if we are to continue (as Christians must) to take Genesis seriously. But why, then, should it be thought that the Genesis material about the creation of men and women is to be protected, and exempted from a similar revisionary understanding? It is in any case impossible to avoid a revisionist interpretation of the creation narratives. Even creationists have a problem with six days. The history of the reception of this text, even in the previous century, leads to the discovery of at least three abandoned views which until recently were asserted as God's holy will revealed in scripture. First, the injunc-tion "Be fruitful and multiply, and replenish the earth, and subdue it" (Genesis 1:28) was made into an argument against the use of contra-ception, even within marriage. Almost all Protestant Christians are now apparently revisionists on contraception, even though no Christian church was prepared to sanction their use until the Lambeth Conference of 1930 (when Anglican bishops were more adventurous). The command to replenish and subdue the earth was once used to justify colonial dominion over native Americans and their land by the British.[39]

That was an imaginative use of the guidebook view of the Bible, involving a "plain sense" interpretation (see chapter 7) of its first chapter by one of the greatest thinkers of the seventeenth century.

Second, a strong argument against divorce, *used by Jesus Christ himself*, is found in the verse "Therefore shall a man leave his father and his mother, and shall cleave unto his wife: and they shall be one flesh" (Genesis 2:24; Matthew 19:6; Mark 10:7–8). Yet almost all Protestants who are unwilling to abandon their biblical literalism about homosexuality become closet revisionists over divorce and remarriage (whatever Jesus might have said). No cleaving necessary among straight couples if things don't work out! Thirdly, all Protestant denominations (as far as I can ascertain) now sanction intentionally childless marriages between fertile couples, full in the face of the divine command "Be fruitful and multiply," and no one even notices. Yet this is clearly contrary to the mainstream historical understanding of that injunction, and contrary to the link between sex and procreation that the *Guide* and Roman Catholic doctrine rightly makes. One could go on. The next verse makes clear God's will that humanity should be vegetarian (Genesis 1:29). Whatever happened to that?

Yes, revisionism, tolerated, encouraged, and even required by the Christian mainstream in so many areas of the Genesis narratives has no place in these verses, for this text has become the foundation for a very new and unstable doctrine, the "complementarity" of the sexes. This term, originally used by physicists and chemists to explain the apparently contrasting behaviors of particles and molecules, has been casually imported into theology to sanctify the alleged incompleteness of men without women and women without men. Apparently "the author of Genesis [which one?] was enabled by God to transcend the limitations of his culture in a way that enabled him to catch a glimpse of God's original intention for the relationship between men and women."[40] At this point the remaining shreds of credulity disintegrate. Genesis 1 tells us that "Both men and women need each other in order to find their fulfilment as human beings."

So now we know. Genesis 1 is about human fulfillment through compulsory heterosexuality. Despite the testimony of historical theology that the image of God is to be understood as something spiritual,[41] the opponents of same-sex couples now discern something quite different: it is about having a sexed body with fixed opposite-sex desires. Suppose we *wanted* to believe this? Wouldn't we need to insert a further, missing premise into the argument, i.e., that the text offers simple universal truths that admit of no, absolutely no, exceptions? From "male and female created he them," and from "Be fruitful and multiply," it is assumed that all males will always desire only females, and conversely; that no one might desire both, and that they will all have children. But the procreative purpose (remember it is OK to be a revisionist about this) is not thwarted if a few, or even some, people of either sex use sex for other reasons than procreation. Most heterosexual couples do this almost every time they have sex. The very existence of men and women who don't fit this convenient pattern should be enough to indicate that the traditional understanding of these texts requires exceptions. (And celibate people are a further exception.) In any case reproduction is something that *species* do. But for species to reproduce successfully it is not necessary for every member of the species to be at it.

Lesbian and gay people are now being exposed to a new line of theological attack. It is not enough to say that the Bible condemns homosexual practice. It is now urged that Genesis 1 precludes their relationships ever being in accordance with God's will. If they think differently they contradict the savage text. There is a double strategy in maintaining the position that the Bible denounces same-sex intimacy. The first part is simply to go on saying so. Endless repetition manipulates hearers (as all campaigners and advertisers know). Frequency also adds authority. Mark Jordan contends that all official Roman Catholic pronouncements about sex have as their intention to *stifle* discussion. They do not offer arguments: they are pernicious ideologies, "instruments of power." Jordan warns, "Responding to ideological discourse requires a rule, not just of suspicion, but of inversion: we should attend not to what the discourse says, but to how it operates."[42] Due attention to ideology also requires not being made to sound like an ideologue oneself when engaging with one. Repetition, then, in the absence of decent argument, soothes as it reinforces. Layfolk, especially if they are gay or lesbian and out, cannot be trusted to think for themselves; nor do they need to for the Magisterium will do it for them, apparently with the requisite sexual experience to speak authoritatively. Added to repetition is the tactic of silence. If scripture settles the argument then there are passages in both Testaments that must on no account be heard lest the Bible be seen to be a more gay-friendly book than it is in the hands of many Christians.

> Now there was leaning on Jesus' bosom one of his disciples, whom Jesus loved. (John 13:23)
>
> Then Peter, turning about, seeth the disciple whom Jesus loved following; which also leaned on his breast at supper, and said, Lord, which is he that betrayeth thee? (John 21:20)

For example, there are four references in the Gospel of John to the disciple whom Jesus loved (13:22–5, 19:26–7, 21:7, 21:20–3). Jesus loved all his disciples, so why was there a particular disciple for whom Jesus had a particular love? What was this love? One detailed examination of these texts yields the conclusion that

> The singling out of one who is loved by Jesus makes clear that some kind of love is at stake other than the love that unites Jesus to the rest of his disciples. The text itself suggests that we should recognize here some form of love that certainly does not contradict the more general love of Jesus for all, but which does set it apart from this general love. A reasonable conclusion is that this difference points us to a different sphere or dimension of love: love characterized by erotic desire or sexual attraction.[43]

Nor are these references the only ones which may suggest a more gay-friendly reading of the Bible than the churches are confident enough in their faith to consider. In the garden of Gethsemane as Jesus was being arrested, Mark's Gospel records "And there followed him a certain young man, having a linen cloth cast about his naked body; and the young men laid hold on him: And he left the linen cloth, and fled from them naked" (Mark 14:51–2). It is plausibly suggested that "we are left with an apparent allusion to the typical recipient of homoerotic attention (the nude youth) in Hellenistic pederastic culture at a decisive moment in the passion of Jesus, and with the suggestion of a particularly close relationship between Jesus and this youth."[44] Jesus, we may speculate, was just the sort of company with whom a sexually exploited young man could relax and feel accepted. The Gospels of Matthew and Luke both record that Jesus healed the servant of a Roman centurion (Matthew 8:5–13; Luke 7:1–10). But Matthew's version uses the term *pais*, or boy, not *doulos* (servant) at 8:13, giving rise to the suggestion that the relation between the centurion and his boy may have included another dimension not normally considered.[45] These are suggestions, nothing more, but they may indicate that the New Testament, and in particular Jesus himself, may be more gay-friendly than conventional readings have been able to acknowledge. Moralists who think the Bible is unambiguous in its condemnation of homosexuality may not be taking the whole Bible seriously enough.

And that is true for the Old Testament too. These books are full of sexual irregularities and deviations (and one of them revels in the uninhibited love-making of an unmarried couple). The easiest way of refuting the claim that the Bible can be our guide to our sexual conduct is a careful reading of it. The long narratives describing the relations between David and Jonathan in 1 and 2 Samuel make little sense unless they were lovers.[46] Imagine a male candidate for ordination today confiding to his bishop that his love for another man was "wonderful, passing the love of women" (2 Samuel 1:26). And if he is an honest Roman Catholic ordinand he will certainly be deemed to "present deep-seated homosexual tendencies" which will "gravely hinder" him "from relating correctly to men and women."[47] Another detailed study concludes that the Ruth and Naomi stories (Ruth 1–4), together with the David and Jonathan stories, "both deal with persons of the same gender loving one another. Because of the passionate romance that characterizes the relationships depicted, and the deep feeling and undying loyalty of the love narrated, these two stories have regularly served as models not only of same-sex but also of cross-sex friendship and lifelong loyalty."[48]

When is Exegesis Homophobic?

At the very least the question arises whether some of the exegesis we have encountered in this chapter is homophobic. A *phobia* is a fear, and fears are sometimes irrational. *Homo*phobia is fear of people who are attracted to the same (*homos*) sex as themselves. Such fear may result in hatred, discrimination, prejudice, and contempt regarding homosexual people. This frequently manifests itself in aggressive behavior against them, and Christians are clearly implicated in this. But that does not mean that those millions of Christians who think the Bible condemns homosexual behavior are homophobes. Many of them are committed to loving God and their neighbor. They wish the Bible did not "say" that homosexuality was wrong. They are in a bind because they find it difficult to accept homosexual people and at the same time to be faithful to "biblical teaching."

On the other hand, the denial of homophobia is suspect. Lack of awareness or complete ignorance or outright denial are deep characteristics of prejudice. Racism, sexism, and anti-Semitism have often been practiced by people who were unaware they were thinking or doing anything wrong. The determination to press ahead with the conventional arguments against homosexual people (which seem to this writer to be embarrassingly weak) raises the question whether a deeper agenda is being followed, or a broader cultural homophobia is being justified. I agree with Dale Martin that "any interpretation of Scripture that hurts people, oppresses people, or destroys people cannot be the right interpretation, no matter how traditional, historical, or exegetically respectable." He is right to say there is no doubt "that the church's stand on homosexuality has caused oppression, loneliness, self-hatred, violence, sickness, and suicide for millions of people."[49]

But at this juncture there is more to say. The issues of the authority of the Bible and the actual use of the Bible, so long kept separate, must be drawn together. Christians must ask what they do with the Bible when the consequences are dire. The argument of this book is that disturbing parallels exist between the treatment of homosexual people and the historical treatment of other minorities. A defective understanding of what the Bible is, and what it is for, has contributed to atrocious outcomes. In order to answer the question about homophobia we need to examine further cases where, as our argument goes, the Bible has become a savage text.

Part II

The Savage Text at Work

In part I, it was claimed that the use of the Bible as a savage text constituted a major deterrent to faith and a major problem for world Christianity. The marginalization of a substantial sexual minority was used to illustrate how implausible and negative arguments are constructed on the isolation of a few biblical texts, on which is built a flimsy edifice of interpretation, judgment, and rejection. Perhaps the churches can get away with these savage uses of scripture because there is a tradition of savage interpretation which has frequently led Christians to act in this way, and which, well into the third millennium, needs to be exorcised from the Body of Christ once and for all? In part II, we will see a similar process in operation in the treatment of other minorities. If we are able to trace similarities of Bible use between adverse judgments made about homosexual people and adverse judgments made about other groups of people, we will have found an additional reason for rejecting the conservative case against them.

3

"Cursed Be Canaan!":
The Bible, Racism, and Slavery

This chapter examines how some Bible passages have been enlisted by Bible readers in support of two great evils: racism and slavery. It then asks how these interpretations happened, and how other, comparably disastrous, interpretations can be avoided.

The Bible and Racism

How has the Bible been used in order to account for the presence in the world of different races of people, especially black people? One key passage is the following:

[18]And the sons of Noah, that went forth of the ark, were Shem, and Ham, and Japheth: and Ham is the father of Canaan. [19]These are the three sons of Noah: and of them was the whole earth overspread. [20]And Noah began to be an husbandman, and he planted a vineyard: [21]And he drank of the wine, and was drunken; and he was uncovered within his tent. [22]And Ham, the father of Canaan, saw the nakedness of his father, and told his two brethren without. [23]And Shem and Japheth took a garment, and laid it upon both their shoulders, and went backward, and covered the nakedness of their father; and their faces were backward, and they saw not their father's nakedness. [24] And

> Noah awoke from his wine, and knew what his younger son had
> done unto him. [25]And he said, Cursed be Canaan; a servant of
> servants shall he be unto his brethren. [26]And he said, Blessed be
> the LORD God of Shem; and Canaan shall be his servant.
> [27]God shall enlarge Japheth, and he shall dwell in the tents of
> Shem; and Canaan shall be his servant. (Genesis 9:18–27)

Readers confronting this passage today will have a hard time making
out who's who and what's what. The story belongs to a strand within
the **Pentateuch** known as **J**, but it is a conflation of more than one
story. In the first story the different peoples of the earth are all said to
have descended from Noah's three sons, Shem, Ham, and Japheth
(God, remember, has just concluded, by drowning, the ecocidal elimi-
nation of all species whatsoever other than those preserved in the Ark
[Genesis 7:21–3]). In the second story the trio are Shem, Japheth, and
Canaan, and Canaan is the youngest son (verse 24). A **redactor** has
tried to harmonize the two stories by adding "Ham the father of
Canaan" at verses 18 and 22.[1] We don't know whether Canaan is
Noah's son or grandson.

What does Canaan do to receive Noah's curse (verse 25)? He comes
across his father, drunk and naked, and seeks the help of his brothers to
get him into bed. That seems filial enough. The actions of Shem and
Japheth appear to indicate some convention about the exposure, even
accidental, of the paternal penis. Fear of ridicule perhaps? Did Canaan
interfere with it? Is that the inference of "what his younger son had
done to him" (verse 24)? Or did he just happen to notice it? Whatever
Canaan did it was bad enough to get cursed. Jewish and Christian
exegetes have puzzled over this narrative ever since it was known.

Next we need to consider a critical and a pre-critical reading of
these stories. A critical reading looks for the sources of the stories, and
tries to see what the editor or editors did with them, and why.
Commentators note aetiological questions being addressed by the
text. For example, how did the earth get its population renewed after
the Flood? What accounts for its diversity? How and when did wine

get made? And why are the native people of Canaan in servitude?[2] A critical reading understands something of the primitiveness of the sources. A pre-critical reading has no access to the tools of investigation, the number of available manuscripts, archaeological findings, and so on, which make a critical reading possible. A critical reading may invoke the theory of "progressive revelation" or "progressive discovery," according to which God was in no hurry to teach us about Godself or anything else, but slowly revealed religious and moral truths over a long period. The guidebook view of the Bible cannot assimilate progressive revelation because that would entail large sections of the guide being unusable. On a pre-critical reading the narrative is to be read much as we might read it today for the first time and without the benefit of any scientific discoveries. The Flood happened. The human race was extirpated, then restored. Because the narrative is about what *God* does (Genesis 9:1–18) (and also what Noah, whom God blesses, does – 9:1), the morality of the story has not usually been questioned. Today the moral questions raised by the story are unavoidable, a sign not of growing unbelief but of growing moral awareness. Leaving aside the Christian conviction that the loving Father of Jesus does not do ecocide, it is not right to curse people, especially if they are blameless, and especially if they are blameless and your own children. (Neither do contemporary Christians hold that curses have performative consequences in the outworking of malevolence.) As the narrative stands, Noah's grandson, Canaan, not Noah's son, Ham, is cursed. This is a morally appalling story, a double injustice. Imagine a grandfather cursing his grandson for his father's misdemeanor (assuming there was one).

Since the stories contain little morally elevating or religiously inspiring material, should we not just move on? Unfortunately we cannot do that because on this text Christians once built the most horrendous justification for racism and enslavement. Savage enough in its surface meanings, it became a savage text which legitimized and sacralized the untold violence done to millions of black people, forced into slavery. From at least 1627 onwards, this text was used to justify the divinely ordained slave status of black people. In an exhaustive study of "the curse of Ham" David Goldenberg observes, "As the Black slave trade moved to England and then America, the Curse of Ham moved with it ... There can be no denying the fact, however, that the Curse made its most harmful appearance in America, and there can be no denying the central role it played in sustaining the slave system. It was *the* ideological cornerstone for the justification of Black slavery."[3] In 1862 a man born in the United States to freed slaves claimed that the divine curse upon black people was the "general, almost universal, opinion in the Christian world." He found it

> in books written by learned men; and it is repeated in lectures, speeches, sermons, and common conversation. So strong and tenacious is the hold which it has taken upon the mind of Christendom, that it seems almost impossible to uproot it. Indeed, it is an almost foregone conclusion, that the Negro race is an accursed race, weighed down, even to the present, beneath the burden of an ancestral malediction.[4]

Here, then, is testimony to the power of the curse of Ham, its acceptance by reasonable white Christians, and its internalization by blacks. It is one of thousands that are available. And here too, in all its sinister unconvincingness and power to crush, is another savage text.

The early chapters of Genesis provided other savage texts for the racists. One of these was "the mark of Cain." The two sons of Adam and Eve quarrel, and Cain kills Abel (Genesis 4:8). Fratricide occurs very early in the Bible. The Lord punishes Cain. Cain appeals to the Lord and, by way of mitigation, Cain enjoys some protection from his angry God: "And the LORD said unto him, Therefore whosoever slayeth Cain, vengeance shall be taken on him sevenfold. And the LORD set a mark upon Cain, lest any finding him should kill him" (Genesis 4:15). Cain's mark, then, enables the Lord to keep a divine eye on Cain. The mark is like an early electronic tagging device. But among the Christian racists, the mark is dark. The mark (the nature of which the Bible does not specify) is Cain's black skin. Here is another savage racist text used by a number of American writers from 1733 onwards.[5] Charles Carroll's two books, *The Negro a Beast* (1901) and

The Tempter of Eve (1902), extended the boundaries of racial contempt yet further. Black people descend from the animals that Noah placed in the ark.[6] Since "God is light, and in him is no darkness at all" (1 John 1:5), God's Adversary *must* be dark. The serpent who tempts Eve in the Garden of Eden (Genesis 3:1–5), and who is identified in Revelation (12:9) as the Devil, *must* be black. Blackness is not simply cursed: it is demonic.

Kelly Douglas records the role of another savage text in bringing about the lynching of a black man in 1899.[7] This time the text was the verse forming the basis of a sermon. It was "Therefore put away from among yourselves that wicked person" (1 Corinthians 5:13), and the sermon based on this text was held to be instrumental in the lynching of a black man by a white Christian mob. Douglas explains how, after the ownership of slaves became illegal, "no longer the property of white people, black life had little or no value in white society." Most of the lynchings "took place in one of the most Christianized parts of the United States," and "many of these violent spectacles of murderous rampage on black bodies took place on Sunday afternoons – as if to have a picnic of black flesh after church."[8]

Is the Bible Racist?

The sheer savagery of the use of the Genesis texts is further underlined by the lack of racist bias in the scriptures. Several racist ideologies are rooted in the Bible, however, and these are our concern since they convert the Bible into a savage text. The Bible is not a racist book. This perhaps surprising claim depends on which of many definitions of racism we accept. The *Oxford English Dictionary* defines racism as "the theory that distinctive human characteristics and abilities are determined by race," and contrasts that with "racialism," which is "belief in the superiority of a particular race leading to prejudice and antagonism towards people of other races, especially those in close proximity who may be felt as a threat to one's cultural and racial integrity or economic well-being."[9] Whether the Bible contains racist ideologies is complicated by the assumption of both Testaments of the basic contrast between Gentiles and Jews. Jews believe themselves to be a people chosen by God, an identifying characteristic which Christians believe they inherit from them. It would take another book to show that the Bible is not racist, that is, that it does not teach that distinctive *human* characteristics and abilities are determined by race. Since it is not part of the overall argument of the book to establish this, I shall refer briefly to a few texts (in addition to those already discussed) that have featured in racist allegations, and to the growing **universalism** within the Bible which is incompatible with racist theories.

Black people in the Bible are "Kushites." Kush is the ancient name for the area of Africa south of Egypt.[10] Moses married a Kushite woman (Numbers 12:1). True, Miriam and Aaron objected, not because Moses' wife was black but because she was no Israelite. Even for this contumacious questioning of Moses' choice of spouse the Lord teaches Miriam a painful lesson by inflicting a disfiguring skin disease upon her (Numbers 12:9).[11] Another text pressed into the service of Christian racism is found in the prophet Amos: "Are ye not as children of the Ethiopian[12] unto me, O children of Israel? saith the LORD" (Amos 9:7). Conventionally Amos compares the imminent destruction of the northern kingdom of Israel with the despised black people of Kush whom his hearers would readily agree deserve to be destroyed for their wickedness. In the service of racism the verse confirms the curse of Ham. Yet an alternative, perhaps dominant, reading of this text among Hebrew scholars holds that "the purpose of the verse is to reject the belief that Israel has a special status before God; the Israelites are just like any other people."[13] If this reading is plausible, a once savage text now has an opposite function altogether – to indicate that the God of Israel has no favorites, not even Israel itself, but is the God of all peoples.

The black woman lover who opens Song of Songs declares "I am black, but comely, O ye daughters of Jerusalem, as the tents of Kedar, as the curtains of Solomon. Look not upon me, because I am black, because the sun hath looked upon me" (Song of Solomon 1:5–6). We shall see in a moment that this too became a savage text, as black skin color becomes part of the Christian **imaginary** of wickedness.

44

The young woman explains her skin color is due to exposure to the sun. Her lover is not at all deterred by the blackness of her beautiful body. He adores her body (and almost every part of it), calling her "fairest among women" (Song of Solomon 1:8). The universalism of the New Testament excludes any particular tribalism, nationalism, or racism in its comprehension of the sheer breadth of the divine love. The biblical account of the giving of the Holy Spirit, which Christians celebrate on Whit Sunday, brings about the miracle whereby "devout men, out of every nation under heaven" were able to hear the Gospel, each "in his own language. And they were all amazed and marvelled" (Acts 2:5, 7). The extensive list of represented nations (Acts 2:9–11) is intended to leave the reader in no doubt about the all-encompassing significance of what was happening. The apostle Peter is quick to emphasize the cosmopolitan and multinational importance of this event. Quoting from the prophet Joel he says: "And it shall come to pass in the last days, saith God, I will pour out of my Spirit upon all flesh" (Acts 2:17; Joel 2:28). The self-giving of God, this time as Holy Spirit, is for all the nations that comprise our common humanity. In a later episode in Acts an Ethiopian, a high-ranking official, is reading the scroll of the prophet Isaiah, and is led to faith by the apostle Philip (Acts 8:26–40). The implications are clear. The official comes from the farthest known point on the earth. Gentiles from the remotest parts of the earth are seeking God, who accepts them. The fledgling Church is charged with showing them the way.

It would be pardonable, but wrong, to think that racism too belonged to the infancy of the human race, that modern racism was an unfortunate abiding trace of an earlier state of wickedness. But while hatred, violence, and war are usually ubiquitous features of ancient and modern civilizations alike, and the causes of war are too complex ever to state exhaustively, the biblical world-view (assuming a single one for the moment) does not endorse racism and is scarcely aware of it. I point this out to emphasize the mind-numbing iniquity of the Christian racists. They are not discovering their racism in the Bible: they are planting it there. I do not offer an argument which says (a) the world-view of the Bible is not racist, therefore (b) Christians should not be racist. Christians have better reasons for not being racist. It is sometimes necessary to distinguish between the biblical world-view and our own. Christians follow Christ, not some biblical world-view. But since the Bible does not have a racist world-view there is no need, when analyzing racism, to distinguish between its world-view and modern world-views.

White, educated, and privileged readers of the Bible need to hear the criticisms of minority black and liberation theologians. One such theologian, Cain Hope Felder, points out that "Throughout the world today, it has become routine for persons of all races to think of biblical characters from Adam and Eve to Noah, Abraham, Isaac, Moses, and even the pharaohs of Egypt, Jesus and his parents, and the entire range of leaders in the Church of the first century as somehow typical Europeans."[14] This is, of course, crazy but true. Felder concurs with the judgment that the scriptures do not condone racism. European Christianity is responsible for that. "The evidence suggests that not only was the biblical ethos without color prejudice, but it neither had any notion of race in the modern sense of the term nor did it care to depict blacks in an unfavorable light."

Neither Ham nor Canaan is identified as black in the narrative. The curse of Canaan, as the text plainly says, is slavery, not blackness. The widely assumed **etymological** association of "Ham" with "dark" has now been exploded.[15] That did not stop countless black people internalizing the feeling of being cursed by God. Most white American Christians in the nineteenth century thought that Ham was the "aboriginal black man." How did the Curse of Ham narrative – an ancient, conflated, implausible, enigmatic, and spiritually vacuous text – come to be a foundation of the edifice of white Christian racism?

Goldenberg's detailed and scholarly work answers that question fully and directly. The Jewish philosopher Philo of Alexandria, a contemporary of Jesus Christ, identifies the blackness of the Ethiopians as evil. The pervasive light/darkness symbolism of the New Testament was always likely to become attached to ethnic meanings. The Church Father Origen (d. 253 CE) interpreted the young black lover of the Song of Songs **allegorically**. Her blackness stands for sin and her

46

Gentile birth: the "daughters of Jerusalem" stand for the Jewish race; her beauty is her conversion to faith in Christ.[16] Origen's interpretation had a huge influence on the theologians who followed him. When Augustine calls the Ethiopians "the remotest and foulest of mankind" he conflates extreme *geographical* distance with extreme *moral* distance, thereby exacerbating moral disapproval of blackness.[17] "In sum, the patristic hermeneutic tradition saw the biblical Ethiopian as a metaphor to signify any person who, not having received a Christian baptism, is black in spirit and without divine light."[18] Goldenberg concludes "The belief that Ham was the ancestor of black Africans, that Ham was cursed by God, and that therefore Blacks have been eternally and divinely doomed to enslavement had entered the canon of Western religion and folklore, and it stayed put well into the twentieth century."[19]

The Bible and Slavery

> Servants, be subject to your masters with all fear: not only to the good and gentle, but also to the froward. For this is thankworthy, if a man for conscience toward God endure grief, suffering wrongfully. For what glory is it, if, when ye be buffeted for your faults, ye shall take it patiently? but if, when ye do well, and suffer for it, ye take it patiently, this is acceptable with God. For even hereunto were ye called: because Christ also suffered for us, leaving us an example, that ye should follow his steps. (1 Peter 2:18–21)

So far we have considered a strand of Christian racism which has its roots in savage texts. But we have not considered the highly ambiguous record of the New Testament regarding slaves. Let us ask the question "what are we to make of those cases in which an honest and historically sensitive reading of the New Testament appears to support practices or institutions that Christians now find morally abominable?"[20] It is possible, indeed charitable, to envisage that the institution of slavery was so fixed and prevalent in the Roman world of the New Testament that no one, certainly neither Peter nor Paul, could have questioned it. The acceptance of slavery in the New Testament is certainly a case where from a modern vantage point the biblical world-view is not simply ambiguous – it is immoral. There are plenty of texts in both Testaments that can be converted into savage ones. But some cannot be. There is also the transforming teaching of Jesus who sees beyond race and class to the coming Reign of God.

Goaded on by the advice above to slaves that they should gladly endure unjust and severe punishment at the hands of cruel masters, let us examine very briefly a few passages about slavery in the next few pages. The point of course is to demonstrate that any approach to this, and to any other, moral issue, which hopes to resolve it on the basis of "what the Bible says," is doomed. It is possible to argue for a softer interpretation of 1 Peter 2 (above) than a surface reading suggests. The writer, on this softer version, knowing that some unjust suffering was inevitable for Christian slaves, relates that suffering to the suffering of Christ, and so encourages them to find the deepest meaning of their suffering in the solidarity of Christ with them. Slaves after all, are being addressed as a vital part of the Christian community. But these sympathetic insights did not contribute much to the text's historical use. Twenty-five years ago the **Mennonite** theologian Willard Swartley produced an unusually honest study, the conclusion of which he admitted was painful to him. Having examined what the Bible says about four issues, slavery, the Sabbath, war, and women,[21] he came to the uncomfortable conclusion that all four issues are undecidable on the basis of textual analysis alone. He found that the guidebook view of the Bible didn't work. It didn't deliver. Swartley quite properly sought divine guidance from the Bible about these matters, and found that opposing positions on each of the issues attracted roughly equal support. His work admirably demonstrates the impossibility of the task it set for itself, namely, to find reliable biblical guidance about the issues it treats. Supporters of the guidebook view need to deal with this finding.

The Bible authorizes slavery. As an Episcopalian bishop in the diocese of Vermont and defender of the right to own slaves in the South of the USA proclaimed (in 1864),

> The Bible's defense of slavery is very plain. St. Paul was inspired, and knew the will of the Lord Jesus Christ, and was only intent on obeying it. And who are we, that in our modern wisdom presume to set aside the Word of God … and invent for ourselves a "higher law" than those holy Scriptures which are given to us "a light to our feet and a lamp to our paths," in the darkness of a sinful and a polluted world?[22]

Readers will note that defenders of compulsory heterosexuality in the twenty-first century use arguments similar in form and content to these. The pro-slavery case is frightening. Swartley helpfully compresses it into four theses. First, it was "divinely sanctioned among the patriarchs."[23] Abraham "was a great slaveowner" (Genesis 12:5, 20:14, 24:35–6, 26:13–14, etc.) and "included them in his property list." "God approved slavery in the time of Joseph." Second, "Slavery was incorporated into Israel's national constitution." The book of Exodus provides laws governing the treatment of slaves: "And if a man smite his servant, or his maid, with a rod, and he die under his hand; he shall surely be punished. Notwithstanding, if he continue a day or two, he shall not be punished: for he is his money" (Exodus 21:20–1). A slaveowner can beat male and female slaves to the point of death because slaves are property (the AV's "money"). But if they die a day or two afterwards the master suffers no punishment himself. The third pro-slavery thesis is that "Slavery was recognized and approved by Jesus Christ and the apostles." They "never said one word against them." The New Testament **Household Codes** assume slavery and the compatibility of the new faith with it (Ephesians 6:5–9; Colossians 3:22–4:1; 1 Peter 2:18–25). And fourth, "Slavery is a merciful institution," not least because millions of black people who would otherwise have perished everlastingly have been brought within reach of the Gospel.[24]

On the other hand, the Bible does not authorize slavery. The case of the abolitionists, found as it was in their sermons, speeches, tracts, and lectures, is summarized in five counter-theses. First, "The so-called slavery of the patriarchs in no way justifies the system of slavery in the USA." Second, "God's deliverance of Israel from slavery in Egypt shows, once and for all, that God hates and condemns slavery." Third, "Hebrew servitude in the time of Moses was voluntary, merciful, and of benefit to the servant; it was not slavery[!]" Fourth, "oppressive slavery did not exist in Israel; God would have roundly condemned it, had it existed." And finally, "Neither Jesus nor the apostles approved" of it.[25]

The score at the end of this hermeneutic contest is a draw. "The Bible says *both* yes and no on slavery."[26] Swartley also allows three possibilities for settling the matter one way or the other. The first is to admit the issue is undecidable on the basis of scripture. Both "sides" on this view owe the duty of respect for each other, for both have attempted to be as faithful to scripture as they know how. This alternative is "troubling" and "should not be too readily dismissed." A second alternative derives from the practice of **Quakers** and Mennonites. "Rather than using the Bible to speak directly to slavery, the basic biblical value structure had so informed their thinking and practice so as to put slavery at odds with their way of life."[27] A third alternative (which will be pursued in a moment) "may be found within the slave community." What do the slaves themselves think of slavery? How do those slaves – and former slaves, and descendants of slaves who have responded to the Gospel – read their Bibles? How has the infinite grace of God impacted upon their real lives?

Reading the Bible after Slavery

Let us now think about these three alternatives. I take it that Christians no longer justify the owning of slaves whatever the Bible says. Even in 1866 the Holy Office of the Roman Catholic Church could say "Slavery itself ... is not at all contrary to the natural and divine law."[28] By the end of the century, though, it was completely forbidden by that Church. Yes, Catholic moral teaching changes, and denial can be one of the signs of change. The argument of this book is that the Bible is constantly in danger of being converted into a savage text by its readers. The Christian majority who believed black people were cursed by God because their supposed ancestor Ham was cursed, and the Christian slave-owners who produced close and detailed arguments in support of slavery provide a further example of savagery. A draw was not a satisfactory outcome in this textual contest. The lives of millions of people lay in the balance. Hindsight doubtless supports the case of the abolitionists, but that case was not won on the basis of textual support alone.

On the issue of slavery the polarization of views was immense. That is why *the extent of agreement* between the adversaries is all the more remarkable. Each side believed the Bible to be the ultimate source of moral wisdom. Each acknowledged the Bible had spoken with regard to slavery. Any abolition of slavery would need to be justified by scripture alone. This is a tedious, near-universal principle governing disputes among Protestants with regard to doctrine, morality, church polity, and much else. They all take the Bible to be the final court of appeal – only no faction among them is able to convince the others of the rectitude of their own favored interpretation. The second alternative is much better. Here two groups of radical Christians did not own slaves because they thought that the practice would be at variance with their Christian way of life. This alternative did not rely on particular biblical texts, although the Great Commandments of Jesus to love God and one's neighbor, and scores like them, were especially formative in Mennonite and Quaker practice. These Christians looked to the Bible to provide them with guiding principles for their form of life. First of these is the principle of charity which "suffereth long, and is kind; charity envieth not; charity vaunteth not itself, is not puffed up" (1 Corinthians 13:4). These Christians read the Old Testament prophets as critics of the unjust Israelite social order. They recognized the violence done to slaves. Their way of life was, and is, the practice of non-violence. Even their enemies are to be loved, as Jesus himself taught (Matthew 5:44).

51

The abolitionists get credit because they "gave priority to theological principles and basic moral imperatives, which in turn put slavery under moral judgment." Swartley thinks the "point we should learn from this is that theological principles and basic moral imperatives should be primary biblical resources for addressing social issues today."[29] I think the description of this position is understated. The Mennonites are said to have adopted "the basic biblical value structure." That phrase begs at least two questions. Is there a basic value structure in the Bible? If so, is there only one? Would we not do better to revert to the conviction that God's final revelation is Christ, to which the scriptures bear witness? Swartley is right to advocate the use of "theological principles and basic moral imperatives" in grappling with social issues, but that admirable position would seem to wreck most forms of biblicism, because priority has to be given to a few texts over the many. Leaving those questions aside, I hold that there are theological possibilities in Christian theology and Christian tradition which can also come to our aid when we are perplexed about life-and-death issues such as this one. Of course Quaker reluctance to draw deeply on theology is precisely their fear of the dogmatism that results from it, leading to violent consequences, not least for the Quakers themselves. The very being of Jesus as "God with us" ("Emmanuel" – Matthew 1:23) allows us to think of God *sharing* our suffering. Christians think Christ's first coming establishes God's solidarity with all women and men of every period, race, and culture as the brothers and sisters of Jesus, his friends. The work of Jesus in the New Testament is to reconcile everything to God (it is far too **anthropocentric** to think that only people are involved, and far too elitist to think that only *some* people are involved). There is no place for the violence of slavery or the social hierarchy that legitimizes its lowest tier. We will say more about the overt theological interpretation of scripture in part III. It is enough to note the peaceable possibilities of theology. Theology can be convincing without being "**dogmatic**."

The third alternative, which attends to the reading of the scriptures of the slaves themselves (by those, that is, who could read) is a suggestion congenial to **liberation theologians**. Liberation theology begins with the voices of oppressed people. A common starting-point is the saying of Jesus who interpreted a verse from the prophet Isaiah (61:1–2) to be fulfilled in his own ministry: "The Spirit of the Lord is upon me, because he hath anointed me to preach the gospel to the poor: he hath sent me to heal the brokenhearted, to preach deliverance to the *captives*, and recovering of sight to the blind, to set at liberty them that are *bruised*" (Luke 4:18, emphases added). The "bruised" are the oppressed, and the captives are slaves. Renita Weems describes how slaves were initially forbidden to learn to read. Slavemasters especially feared the revolutionary potential of the scriptures, so knowledge of them was mediated through the slavemasters themselves, and the black churches set up for them.[30] Generally speaking, slaves were rightly wary of any interpretation of the Gospel that oppressed them. Weems explains: "What the slavemasters did not foresee, however, was that the very material they forbade the slaves from touching and studying with their hands and eyes, the slaves learned to claim and study through the powers of listening and memory."[31] For Afro-Americans, continues Weems, "it is not texts per se that function authoritatively. Rather, it is reading strategies, and more precisely, *particular* readings that turn out, in fact, to be authoritative."[32]

The self-understanding of the slaves in the light of scripture is therefore very different from the fundamentalism of the present day. One difference is that for the Afro-American churches the Bible is not one undifferentiated, inspired Word. The authority of the Bible was not to be found in some prior dogma about what the Bible is. Its authority lies in its power to change lives, to offer hope, to point to the liberating power of Jesus. Afro-American Christians had what Kelly Douglas calls a "hermeneutic of appropriation." Yes, they *did* use scripture selectively. Who doesn't? "[W]hat did not accord with black people's own aspirations regarding the treatment of their black bodies was not appropriated as authoritative within the black faith tradition. This means that not everything written in the Bible was granted authority."[33] For example, "the exodus saga concerning God's liberation of the Israelites from bondage was given normative authoritative status, while the Pauline Epistles, particularly with their directives for 'slaves to submit to their masters,' were not." Rather, black Christians had a "theological core" of "equality, justice and love," and they used the Bible in its service.

The second and third alternatives will be developed in the final chapter. The argument will be that the "theological core" is Jesus Christ, so any principles either of practice or of interpretation will need to be derived from him in one way or another. But suppose we allow some objective meaning to the biblical text (that slaves should suffer cheerfully, say), we still need to interpret the text, to engage with it in a deep way, hoping against appearances, that for example it does not endorse the suffering of slaves, or the institution of slavery, or the hierarchy of God–angels–rulers–men–women–children–slaves that oppresses everyone except the powerful. This is surely obvious (and the obvious surely needs to be stated). It is also obvious that Protestants have spawned scores of different interpretations of different texts, too many of them savage. A further conclusion too cannot be avoided: a single authoritative interpretation (say, of the slave texts we considered earlier) is impossible to find. As Weems shrewdly observes, "After all, the history of Protestantism aptly points out that different readings (and hence interpretations) of the one fixed text, the Bible, have existed simultaneously."[34] The sheer, unregulated diversity of Protestant interpretation of the Bible had an ironic consequence. Slaves, well aware of the discordant disunity of Protestant interpretations, concluded that they too had the same freedom of interpretation of the scriptures as their teachers. Vincent Wimbush comments:

> The lesson that the Africans learned from these evangelicals was not only that faith was to be interpreted in light of the reading of the Bible, but also that each person had freedom of interpretation of the Bible. Given differences between individuals and different religious groups, the Africans learned that they, too, could read "the Book" freely. They could read certain parts and ignore others.[35]

The refusal of oppressive readings of scripture is an essential human defensive reaction to religious bigotry and to the misuse of the sacred mantle that still wraps itself around religious discourse. It is a matter of life and death that such interpretations be refused. Believers throughout the world can learn from the refusal of slaves to see themselves as their masters, aided by their savage text, saw them. "The emotional, psychological, and religious health of African American women has been directly related to their refusal to hear the Bible uncritically and their insistence upon applying what one might call an aural hermeneutic."[36]

In this chapter I have drawn attention to the way the Bible was used by white Christians to condone and justify the violence done to slaves. It would take a further chapter to chart the contribution of these savage texts to the history of *apartheid* in South Africa. The American **black theologian** James Cone has recently drawn attention to what he alleges to be the complete silence within white theology about racism. Racism, he says, "is America's original sin. It is its most persistent and intractable evil. Though racism inflicts massive suffering, few American theologians have even bothered to address [it]."[37] His reasons for the alleged failure to engage include white guilt, fear of black rage, and of the costly redistribution of resources that justice demands. As a white European it would be presumptuous to join in this argument, except perhaps to say that if Cone is right, a further reason for white silence about black racism has been a reluctance to own the history of Bible use that has supported it. When the manipulated texts of scripture are implicated in such vast suffering, it is easy to attempt to forget them. Yet precisely because millions of Christians continue to use the Bible in ways similar to the Christian racists, but with different targets, it is important to eliminate savage texts from Christianity altogether.

It is also important to affirm that there is much in the Bible that cannot be enlisted in support of slavery. An argument is available that the teaching of Jesus about the reversal of social hierarchies is too radical for a hierarchical church ever to be able to operate. Christ himself compared the Roman enslavement of peoples with his own movement, where "whosoever will be great among you, let him be your minister; And whosoever will be chief among you, let him be your servant" (Matthew 20:26–7). His own way of crucifixion indicated the path to follow. Crusading Christians, many of whom were evangelical Christians, were in the vanguard against the slave trade.[38] In Britain that movement was led by William Wilberforce, and the 200th anniversary of his achievement was being celebrated as this book was being written. The point is not to denigrate the Christian faith but to isolate a strand within it which elevates the text of scripture above the practice of costly love, social justice, and the "fruit of the Spirit" (Galatians 5:22) which Jesus Christ makes possible. Who knows how many Christians did actually believe God had cursed black people? Such belief cannot be reconciled with the Crucified God of Christian faith. When Christians find such dangerous and destructive nonsense in their holy book, they have shown they are incapable of reading it for the purpose for which it was given.

4

"The Great Day of Wrath": The Bible and the End

This chapter sets itself two tasks. First, it strongly suggests that the level, and the persistence, of violence throughout the Bible, but especially in the Old Testament, may have desensitized Christians throughout the history of Christianity to the horror of it. We may have become gravely inured to its apparent inevitability. From Genesis to Revelation there is violence. Its omnipresence may have obscured from the eyes of the faithful the sight of the crucified Nazarene, whose death, according to appropriate Christian theology, draws the sting of violence and so brings it to an end. The violent treatment by Christians of heretics and religious opponents is a strong argument against the moral truth of Christianity (an issue to be addressed in part III). Second, the bulk of the chapter shows how millions of disaster-inclined conservative Christians are using a particular genre of biblical writing, **apocalyptic**, in order to justify violence and the threat of violence on a global scale. How? By associating it with the ultimate bloody triumph of good over evil which features in the book of Revelation. The relation between the Bible, global politics, and Western militarism is explained.

"Man of War" or "Prince of Peace"?

> And it repented the LORD that he had made man on the earth, and it grieved him at his heart. And the LORD said, I will destroy man whom I have created from the face of the earth; both man, and beast, and the creeping thing, and the fowls of the air; for it repenteth me that I have made them. (Genesis 6:6–7)

The violence of the Old Testament need cause Christians little moral anxiety. It can be largely explained by the circumstances in which, probably beginning around the thirteenth century BCE, the Israelites escaped from Egypt and the 12 tribes of Israel waged a brutal war in the name of their God against the inhabitants of Canaan, and won. The primitiveness of this conquest, the violent and ruthless means of its achievement, and the vicious, tribal character of the God to whose action victory was ascribed, are written all over the early books of the Old Testament. Gradually monotheism became established, and the belief in one God as Creator led to a more universal and inclusive outlook. The moral character of this God as one of mercy and even compassion began to dawn upon the religious consciousness with increasing intensity. Religious scholars refer to the Axial Period (roughly from the eighth to the second centuries BCE) as a time when throughout the known world – China, Asia, Palestine, the Mediterranean region, Egypt – there was a notable and lasting advance in religious, philosophical, and spiritual traditions. The hypothesis that the human consciousness of God needed to, and did, develop is a sound one (provided it does not assume the crass liberal optimism of the nineteenth and early twentieth centuries). This development has been called "progressive revelation" or "progressive discovery." **John Calvin** had a similar thought when he spoke of "accommodation." God, he taught, "accommodates" Godself to our limited capacities for understanding.[1] The human race cannot receive what it cannot understand, so revelation deepens in accordance with the human capacity to recognize it.

Unfortunately this option is not open to those millions of conservative Christians who take the "guidebook view" of the Bible and who regard it as the undifferentiated Word of God. They are more conservative than Calvin himself was about the Bible. It is not open to them to accept much of the Old Testament as purporting to be ancient history or "chronicle" (as two long books are called) which tells us about the long, bloody story of Hebrew religious identity. If the "plain sense"[2] of a biblical passage is the only or primary sense that is to be accorded to it, then the harmful fiction is maintained that God is still "speaking" to us through these vicious and vindictive narratives. It is vitally necessary for Christian faith to distinguish between the vengeful tribal god of the early Old Testament and the God who is revealed as self-giving Love through Jesus Christ. The savagery of these texts is not the issue before us. The issue is how exposure to these texts may both distort the character of the triune God in the minds of their readers, and habituate them towards the inevitability of violence, especially in the treatment of opponents.

We have already met the god who floods the earth. This god seems far removed from the God who "so loved the world, that he gave his only begotten Son, that whosoever believeth in him should not perish, but have everlasting life" (John 3:16). Two hundred years of looking for the ark that Noah built, dating "the Flood," arguing about its extent, and so on, have detracted from the graver problem of the moral enormity of the actions of this angry, capricious, god who lashes out at everything he has made (and which a few verses ago was "very good" – Genesis 1:31) and drowns it. This god clearly did not foresee the extent of human wickedness (which he also seems unable to prevent), and he seems as annoyed with himself as with the creature he made in his image. According to Genesis 3 it was our first human *parents* who sinned. What did the global population of animals, reptiles, and birds do to deserve mass extinction?

The story of the exodus of Hebrew slaves from Egypt (in the book of Exodus) is one of the roots of Hebrew identity (see Deuteronomy 26:5–9) and is commemorated during the annual Jewish holiday of Pesach (Passover). This story of deliverance inspired Christian slaves in the modern period to look for their deliverance, while the narrative still inspires Liberation Theology today. Yet is the moral character of this liberating God beyond reproach? The Lord sends plagues upon the Egyptians (Exodus 7–12) as an encouragement to the Pharaoh to let the Israelites go, but sending plagues became such good sadistic sport that the Lord delays the Israelites' departure so he can have some more fun at the Egyptians' expense. The Lord announces to Moses, "I have hardened his heart, and the heart of his servants, that I might shew these my signs before him: And that thou mayest tell in the ears of thy son, and of thy son's son, what things I have wrought ["how I have made sport" – RSV] in Egypt, and my signs which I have done among them; that ye may know how that I am the LORD." Was it really necessary for the Lord to murder all firstborn children through-out Egypt (and even the firstborn of cattle [Exodus 11:5]) when the Israelites escaped? The God of the Exodus is definitely a child-killer. And he can't tell his own people from the Egyptians either. Is the Lord really so limited in the power of recognition that he requires blood-stained doorposts to avoid killing his own people as he goes about on his vindictive night-time killing spree (Exodus 12:22–3)? Yes, he "passes over" the bloody doors of the Israelites as he (or his "destroyer" [Exodus 12:23]) goes about his death-dealing mission. But is this God not God of the Egyptians too? "The LORD is a man of war: the LORD is his name," sang the Israelites (Exodus 15:3) after the pursu-ing Egyptian army drowned. But according to the prophet Isaiah (9:6) the Lord will also send the Prince of Peace, whom Christians understand to be Jesus Christ. "Man of War" and "Prince of Peace" are ultimately different names for the same, one God. But the moral visions that give rise to these names cannot be regarded as morally equivalent.

And the Lord behaves like a man of war as the Israelites possess Canaan, the land "flowing with milk and honey" (e.g., Exodus 3:8) but which, unfortunately, was already occupied by different peoples who are ruthlessly exterminated in the land-grabbing that follows under the leadership of Joshua. "The LORD hearkened to the voice of Israel, and delivered up the Canaanites; and they utterly destroyed them and their cities" (Numbers 21:3). The Lord does not merely fight on behalf of the Israelites. The Lord *provokes* massacres. The Lord "hardened" the spirit of the king of Heshbon, "and made his heart obstinate" (Deuteronomy 2:30). That is why the king refuses to give the Israelite army safe passage through his territory. What happens?

> And the LORD our God delivered him before us; and we smote him, and his sons, and all his people. And we took all his cities at that time, and utterly destroyed the men, and the women, and the little ones, of every city, we left none to remain: Only the cattle we took for a prey unto ourselves, and the spoil of the cities which we took. (Deuteronomy 2:33–5)

This is Holy War, the biblical version. There is nothing here of the compassion of Jesus for children (Matthew 18:1–6). They are slaughtered without mercy, just like the firstborn of the Egyptians. Cattle are worth more than children – they can be spared. The commandment not to steal is apparently suspended during the looting that follows. Indeed in another **pogrom** narrative, even sparing the cattle from slaughter is the sign of fatal weakness and disobedience:

> Thus saith the LORD of hosts, I remember that which Amalek did to Israel, how he laid wait for him in the way, when he came up from Egypt. Now go and smite Amalek, and utterly destroy all that they have, and spare them not; but slay both man and woman, infant and suckling, ox and sheep, camel and ass ... And Saul smote the Amalekites from Havilah until thou comest to Shur, that is over against Egypt. And he took Agag the king of the Amalekites alive, and utterly destroyed all the people with the edge of the sword. But Saul and the people spared Agag, and the best of the sheep, and of the oxen, and of the fatlings, and the lambs, and all that was good. (1 Samuel 15:2–3, 7–9)

Unfortunately for Saul, sparing the animals counted as rebellion against the Lord. Samuel explains to Saul that his "rebellion is as the

61

sin of witchcraft" (15:23) for which the Lord withdraws his support for Saul as king. Yes, godly extermination now permits no exceptions, not even animals. The devout Samuel, the popular subject of Christian sermons on obedience to the call of God (1 Samuel 3) did his best to make amends and please the Lord. He "hewed Agag in pieces before the LORD in Gilgal" (15:33).

There is nauseous violence on many pages of the Pentateuch and the books of Samuel, Kings, and Chronicles (which is not to deny there is also much of religious value). The argument of this book is not directed against any of the violence in particular. These biblical books reflect the violence and religion of their times. Who is surprised at their savagery? They teach us who the Jewish people are and what begins to happen to them. They are Jewish scriptures long before they become Christian scriptures too. Without them the arrival of the Messiah and the universalistic message of the Kingdom of God to the Gentiles make no sense. Without the law of Moses, Gospel teaching and the theology of the New Testament are unintelligible. No, the argument is directed against the sacralization of these texts beyond the sense they make of Jesus. And that remains Christianity's enduring problem.

Once the moral enormity of these texts is undergirded by the dogma of divine authorship, or thought to represent the Christian God speaking to us, or to be for us the Word of God, then ideology has already taken over. The guidebook view of the Bible asserts itself, and Christ is no longer needed as the lens through which Christians read the Hebrew scriptures. Christians must respect that Jews will read the Jewish scriptures differently from the way Christians read them. Once Christians adopt a meaning-frame that is independent of Christ, the pious soul is easily tricked into treating Saul, or Samuel, or David, or whoever, as heroes or role models. We don't need them. Isn't Jesus sufficient? The best antidote to thinking that the Bible is the Word of God is to read it carefully. Graver perils await sincere Christians whose misplaced faith in the Bible equals or even exceeds their faith in Christ. They are bound to think that God has just the character that the Bible really does say God has. And that inevitably detracts from and denies the character of God that has been made known in Christ.

That God is *not* vengeful, capricious, a man of war, punitive, murderous, particularist, jealous, ecocidal, cynical, scheming, and so on.
The Word of God ideology is bound to conflate, fatally, the words of
scripture with the Word made flesh. One is divine and human; the
other is all too human, and not divine. All Christians have a stake in
showing that parts of the Bible are utterly wrong about the character
of God. At some point it is necessary to decide between the all-giving,
all-loving God and the ideology of the book.

In what ways, then, are these texts "savage" as that term has been carefully defined (see chapter 1 above)? They can become savage in three
ways. First, as just indicated, they compromise the character of God.
A savage god springs from the pages of his Word. That is a different
reading from one that listens attentively to what the Hebrew Bible tells us
of the coming of Christ, of all that was necessary for humankind to prepare
to receive him, and of our human need of him. Second, biblical examples
of savagery have been used to justify violence, especially violence shown
by Christians to Christians. Oliver Cromwell is a good example. He justified his massacres at Drogheda and Wexford in Ireland in 1649 on the
basis of the murder of the Amalekites in 1 Samuel 15.[3] (Eight years before,
Catholics had slaughtered hundreds of Protestant civilians in Ulster.)

But third, there may be a cumulative impact upon the religious
consciousness of all Christians who self-define as "Bible-believing"
which is potentially harmful to them. The impact is analogous to the
watching of violent DVDs. In a tiny number of cases individuals rep-
licate or act out scenes that have disturbed or excited them. The more
serious problem is the likely desensitization to violence that exposure
to the many different media forms of it may inculcate among viewers.
With Bible readers a similar danger lurks. It is too easy for Christians,
when they disagree with each other, with their political and religious
leaders, and with people of non-Christian faiths, to start cursing and
fighting each other (or in the present Episcopalian case declaring
impaired communion with one another). The overriding Christian
ethical response wherever there is disagreement is to love one's adversary as one would love oneself. But the ever-present irruption of difference into violence brings the sense of an inevitability of conflict

among and between Christians, and between Christians and people of other faiths. The soul is corroded by the vista of religiously sanctioned conflict. The ethos of violence overcomes the non-violence which Christ came to proclaim and to set firmly in our midst.

"Rapture" or Rupture?

There is another type of savage text which issues in the justification of real, injurious, global, political violence, and that is the use made of apocalyptic. The Apocalypse is the Greek name given to the last book in the Bible, Revelation. The term literally means "lifting of the veil." Apocalyptic is a type of literature, much of it extra-biblical, which claims to be able to see into the way the world will end. There are apocalyptic sections of each of the synoptic Gospels,[4] and in two of Paul's early letters.[5] In the next few pages the veil will be lifted from the dangerous lunacy of a populist and enormously influential reading of biblical apocalyptic literature, "millennialism." In the hands of millions of evangelical Christians, some of them politically influential, the entire genre of apocalyptic will be seen to undermine any prospect of world peace, or environmental conservation. Apocalyptic must now be added to the growing list of savage texts that distort Christian faith and damage it irreparably. Millennialism ruptures the Christian hope in the ultimate triumph of good over evil. It is the counsel of despair, legitimized by savage apocalyptic texts. It dissipates the Christian virtue of hope (1 Corinthians 13:13), replaces it with savage prediction, and sacralizes its doom-mongering with biblical authority.

Let us start with a belief common to all the basic Christian creeds. Christ will come again. Most Christians believe that what God brought to a partial or **proleptic** completion in Christ at the time of his incarnation, crucifixion, and resurrection – victory over violence, sinfulness, injustice, lack of love, and so on – God will bring to a final completion when the world is finally rid of all these things. In the New Testament this conviction is meshed with three immediate factors: first, the belief that Christ would come again very quickly *in the lifetime of the disciples* *and the early Church*; second, the cataclysmic destruction of the temple in Jerusalem in 70 CE by the Romans, which did *not* precipitate divine intervention; and third, the conviction, best expressed in Revelation, that the Roman empire was evil, and would have to be overthrown before God's final purposes could ever be achieved.

Paul's early view, dated 50 CE, about 20 years after the crucifixion of Jesus, is clear:

> But I would not have you to be ignorant, brethren, concerning them which are asleep, that ye sorrow not, even as others who have no hope. For if we believe that Jesus died and rose again, even so them also which sleep in Jesus will God bring with him. For this we say unto you by the word of the Lord, that we which are alive and remain unto the coming of the Lord shall not prevent[6] them which are asleep. For the Lord himself shall descend from heaven with a shout, with the voice of the archangel, and with the trump of God: and the dead in Christ shall rise first: Then we which are alive and remain shall be caught up together with them in the clouds, to meet the Lord in the air: and so shall we ever be with the Lord. (1 Thessalonians 4:13–17)

Some Christians, nearly 20 years before the first Gospel (Mark) was written, are already anxious that some of their number have died before the Second Coming or **Parousia** of Christ. Paul reassures them that, because Jesus rose from the dead, they too will rise from the dead, and no advantage will accrue to those Christians who are alive at Christ's second coming. In fact the dead will be accorded priority for they will rise first.[7] He clearly numbers himself among "we which are alive and remain."[8]

We must bracket out most of the troubling features of this passage (such as the status of those who "sleep," the possible reconstitution of long-decomposed bodies, the spatial location of earth and heaven, the presence of angels, and so on) in order to concentrate upon one detail, the expectation of Christ's imminent return. Paul's ethical outlook and advice are predicated on this assumption (1 Corinthians 7:29). Indeed *even Jesus Christ may have expected someone called "the Son of*

Man" to arrive in the lifetime of his disciples. That is Mark's clear suggestion (Mark 9:2). Now this ought to be a problem for the biblicists. It could hardly be more obvious that Paul was wrong about this, even as Mark's Jesus may have been wrong. Other parts of the New Testament are more reticent about speaking of times and dates ("It is not for you to know the times or the seasons, which the Father hath put in his own power" [Acts 1:7]). Still other parts are clearly embarrassed about the indefinite postponement of the Parousia (2 Peter 3:3–4), and explain its delay as held back to allow increased time for repentance (2 Peter 3:9). Paul (and the early Church) was plainly wrong about this imminent expectation. This ought to be a big problem for all Bible readers who think that scripture or its authors, or its divine Author, cannot err.

So Christ is coming again, and his arrival has been indefinitely postponed. That merely increases speculation about the timing, *and about what happens next* in the cosmic scheme of things. At this juncture the literal reading of apocalyptic texts and their determined application to contemporary events generates an alarming political scenario. The New Testament God is able to tell who God's real followers are. There is no need in the new dispensation for blood on the doorposts as an aid to recognition. With cosmically heard background music Christian believers, living and dead, will be removed from the earth. There is a saying of Jesus that is often applied to the event, one which underlines the suddenness and the unpredictability of its happening. "Then shall two be in the field; the one shall be taken, and the other left. Two women shall be grinding at the mill; the one shall be taken, and the other left" (Matthew 24:40; Luke 17:34–5). The series of "Left Behind" novels has exploited this scenario,[9] and the video game of that name was at the time of writing attracting much controversial and successful publicity.[10] These novels are full of apocalyptic violence from beginning to end, some of it delivered by God, some of it by human machines and wars. This sudden experience of being snatched out of the world is known among the cognoscenti as "the Rapture" (not to be confused with the New York post-punk rock band of that name). The name itself is awkward. "Rapture" and "rape" derive from the same word (*harpazō*: to seize, snatch away, carry off). It is the verb Paul uses and which is translated as "caught up" in the verse "shall be caught up together with them in the clouds." This seizure of Christians is also thought likely to occur just prior to some precipitous disaster, in order for it to be a genuine rescue. But which disaster? And what then? Will the world really be that much worse a place now that the people believing such things have been forcibly removed from it? Apparently so.

Christians who take these apocalyptic sayings literally attempt to construct a chronology of the end times. Jehovah's Witnesses, Seventh Day Adventists, Christadelphians, and countless fundamentalist and evangelical groups all have their own take on "the last things." They are undeterred by the warning of Jesus that "It is not for you to know the times or the seasons." An early problem is the relation of the Rapture to another cataclysmic event, "the Great Tribulation," a term found in Matthew's and Mark's Gospels and attributed to Jesus. Is the Rapture before the Great Tribulation, or after it?

Great Tribulation or American Tribalism?

For then shall be great tribulation, such as was not since the beginning of the world to this time, no, nor ever shall be. And except those days should be shortened, there should no flesh be saved: but for the elect's sake those days shall be shortened ... Immediately after the tribulation of those days shall the sun be darkened, and the moon shall not give her light, and the stars shall fall from heaven, and the powers of the heavens shall be shaken: And then shall appear the sign of the Son of man in heaven: and then shall the tribes of the earth mourn, and they shall see the Son of man coming in the clouds of heaven with power and great glory. And he shall send his angels with a great sound of a trumpet, and they shall gather together his elect from the four winds, from one end of heaven to the other. (Matthew 24:21–2; 29–31[11])

The Great Tribulation seems here to take place prior to the Rapture. The "elect" endure it. It is shortened for their sake. Only after it is shortened does the Rapture occur. Paul seems to know nothing of the Great

Tribulation, nor does the author of 2 Peter. For him "the day of the Lord will come as a thief in the night; in the which the heavens shall pass away with a great noise, and the elements shall melt with fervent heat, the earth also and the works that are therein shall be burned up" (3:10). But the harmonizers of apocalyptic have a bigger problem to deal with – the thousand-year rule of Christ, or "the Millennium." In order to understand the difficulties our modern apocalyptists encounter, it will be necessary to quote from a chapter of Revelation at some length.

One of the later visions in Revelation is of "an angel come down from heaven, having the key of the bottomless pit and a great chain in his hand. And he laid hold on the dragon, that old serpent, which is the Devil, and Satan, and bound him a thousand years, And cast him into the bottomless pit" (Revelation 20:1–3). During this millennial rule the Christian martyrs "lived and reigned with Christ." In this vision there are two resurrections, not one. During the millennial rule the Christian dead stay dead, or rather "asleep." Only the Christian martyrs share Christ's reign: "The rest of the dead lived not again until the thousand years were finished. This is the first resurrection." (Revelation 20:5)

The first resurrection happens at the end of the millennial rule. And then, "when the thousand years are expired, Satan shall be loosed out of his prison, And shall go out to deceive the nations which are in the four quarters of the earth, Gog and Magog, to gather them together to battle" (Revelation 20:7–8). The Devil's armies are seen to have

> compassed the camp of the saints about, and the beloved city: And fire came down from God out of heaven, and devoured them. And the devil that deceived them was cast into the lake of fire and brimstone, where the beast and the false prophet are, and shall be tormented day and night for ever and ever. (Revelation 20:9–10)

After this the "second resurrection" occurs, a general resurrection of the dead where everyone gets judged: "And death and hell were cast into the lake of fire. This is the second death. And whosoever was not found written in the book of life was cast into the lake of fire" (Revelation 20:14–15).

It takes a determined biblicism to construct a real-time chronology on the basis of these strange, almost hallucinogenic visions. Yet that is exactly what millions of Protestant Christians, mainly in the United States of America, are doing. Other catastrophic events also need to be included in the scenario. There are seven seals to be broken open,[12] and four colored horses to be let loose (Revelation 6:1–8:1). Seven trumpets are to be sounded (8:2–11:19) each ushering in various catastrophes. There are seven visions (12–14) and seven bowls or "vials" (15–16) which "pour out … the wrath of God upon the earth" (16:1), leading to the battle of Armageddon (16:16) and the destruction of "the great city," Babylon (16:19–18:24). These visions are accompanied by disasters which make the temptation to relate them to contemporary natural and cosmic events irresistible. There are world wars, famine, plagues of locusts, massive earthquakes (causing tsunamis?), darkening of the sun (pollution? CO_2 in the atmosphere? nuclear winter?), a burning mountain (volcanoes? asteroids?), the burning of large parts of the earth (droughts? global warming? desertification?), polluted water and plague (AIDS?). As we shall see, these events are "mapped on" to contemporary global politics, with savage, indeed devastating, effects.

There are two main versions of the Millennial Rule, and arguments rage through various denominations and websites about each. According to one, premillennialism (or **dispensationalism**), Christ will come again before the millennium, and will literally reign on the earth for a thousand years with his martyred saints at his second coming, in accordance with Revelation 21. According to a different version, postmillennialism, Christ's second coming occurs after the thousand-year reign. (The terms themselves are misleading. They refer to the Parousia not to the millennium. "Premillennial" locates the second coming of Christ before the millennium; "postmillennial" locates it afterwards.) Michael Northcott explains, the

early American settlers and divines were *post*millennialists, which is to say that they believed that in building a godly commonwealth in the

New World they were ushering in the millennial rule of the saints on earth *after* which they believed Christ would return as judge of the earth. The term postmillennialism is used to distinguish this older variety of millennial belief from *pre*millennialism which now predominates in American religion ... Premillennialists believe that the just judgement will happen *before* the millennial rule of the saints.[13]

It might still be possible to hold that these eschatological speculations, though weird, are harmless, the private musings of pious Protestant individuals, whose traditions have cut them off from more satisfying, demanding, and authentic forms of Christianity. (I recall endless conversations in my teen years with **Plymouth Brethren** and Baptists about the Great Tribulation, remaining respectfully silent in the presence of wise elders as their prognostications unfolded.) I did not realize then that vastly more is now at stake than private, harmless speculation. The most powerful nation on earth is increasingly in the grip of these apocalyptic world-views, and they are deployed, cynically and ruthlessly, to advance the imperial interests of the United States. They must be added to our growing list of savage texts.

In conservative United States Protestantism there has been a marked shift of emphasis from the historical postmillennialism of that country to a premillennialism which brings "a much darker perspective on the history of America, and of the planet." The Civil War and its aftermath caused a "fading" of the premillennial "dream," [14] and its successor has enjoyed a renewed prominence from the 1970s to the present time. "Premillennialists" think the Great Tribulation is happening now, and that evidence for it is found in the various threats to global peace and stability, particularly as it affects the affluent way of life in the USA. Only after the dreadful chaos of these events will Christ return in order to establish his millennial rule. While the earlier view spawned "a progressive march of humanity towards the kingdom," the later view accepts as inevitable that there will be suffering, world war, poverty, famine, environmental degradation, global pollution. Now the Bible provides divine **foreknowledge** and **foreordination** of most or all of our present ills. Should the foreign policy of the United States require the use of nuclear weapons, well, conflagration belongs to the end times anyway. Ronald Reagan, prior to his presidency in 1971 proclaimed that "the day of Armageddon isn't far off ... Ezekiel says that fire and brimstone will be rained upon the enemies of God's people. That must mean that they'll be destroyed by nuclear weapons."[15] Such rhetoric is commonplace among senior Republicans and their advisors. If economic greed should render the environment less habitable, well, devastation is inevitable before the Lord returns. It is helpful to business that the heads of global corporations should internalize these calumnies against humankind, all coming from God's Word. If the saturation of world food markets with subsidized grain or rice from the USA pitches a few hundred thousand more people into famine, well, famine is inevitable too. Scripture says so. Liberal Christianity is an irrelevance. What is necessary is to preach the gospel to all nations before the end comes (Matthew 24:14) and the Rapture removes the faithful. Christians who do not read the scriptures in the same way, and who treat all women and men as the precious children of God belong to an **apostate** church which God has also foreseen and foretold. The idea of "great tribulation" has attached itself to the economic interests of the US empire as part of the apocalyptic vision that endorses the activities of a powerful elite. Tribulation endorses tribalism. A minority of evangelical Christians in the USA dissent from these views,[16] but most do not.

The dispensationalists see the Middle East as the flashpoint of the end times. "The beloved city" that features in the Armageddon narrative is Jerusalem. The conversion of Jews is assured – "blindness in part is happened to Israel, until the fullness of the Gentiles be come in. And so all Israel shall be saved" (Romans 11:25–6). The conversion of the Jews to Christianity was the reason why Oliver Cromwell, during the Protectorate in England (1653–9), allowed Jewish people back into England after their expulsion, which had lasted since 1290. How could the Church set about the conversion of the Jews, which scripture foretold, if there were no Jews to convert?[17] He too was a dispensationalist who would have enjoyed the "Left Behind" daily e-mail bulletins. The creation of a Jewish state in Palestine in 1948 was

71

thought to create the conditions for the beginning of the end, and ever since events to do with Jerusalem, such as the Six Day War in 1967, have been thought to presage the final conflagration between God and Satan, which in Revelation is called Armageddon (16:16). In Hal Lindsey's film *The Late Great Planet Earth*, the former Soviet Russia is identified with Gog and Magog. China is the "yellow peril" that will emerge from beyond "the great river Euphrates" (Revelation 9:16). She will need to be dealt with by whatever means are appropriate. The European Economic Community was seen as a threat to the empire of the United States, a revived Roman empire. Dispensationalists, explains Northcott, are "deeply critical of international gatherings of nations, and especially the United Nations and the European Union, which they view as indicative of end time accounts of a pernicious world government that will eventually invite the Antichrist to head it up."[18] During the presidency of Ronald Reagan, "More than one-third of Americans believed at the time in the inevitability of a nuclear conflagration, seeing it as part of a divine plan for the end of history which no one nation could do anything to prevent."[19] The war in Iraq was aimed at strengthening the position of the United States and Israel in the region. Should Islamist opposition erupt into a third world war, so what?

It must be stressed that not all Christians in the United States think along these lines. None of my Christian friends in the USA does. Many of the critics of the empire of the United States live there. Criticism of another country is easier than appreciation. Nonetheless I concur with Northcott's conclusion that "The US corporate elite increasingly see themselves as engaged in a planetary war for the maintenance of their own prosperity and way of life, and for the directing of all human history to American ends."[20] I think his theological judgment is sound that the purpose of Revelation was to expose the evil of the Roman empire and to place confidence in the non-violent kingdom of Christ. What these savage texters have done is to convert apocalyptic into its very opposite. "It is a tragic deformation of biblical apocalyptic that in America for more than two centuries millennialism, far from unveiling empire, has served as a sacred ideology that has cloaked the expansionary tendencies of America's ruling elites."[21] Their religion is profoundly dangerous. Linked to global capitalism, confident in the moral and religious right of the United States to rule the world (and maintain "full spectrum dominance" over it),[22] strenuous academic and religious unmasking of it is urgently required. Luther and Calvin would be appalled at what Protestantism has become. Luther was reluctant to use the book of Revelation because he thought that "Christ is not taught or known in it." Later he (and Calvin) found it useful to identify the Pope with the Antichrist (and the Catholic Cardinal Bellarmine identified "the angel of the bottomless pit" [Revelation 9:11] with Luther and Lutheranism).[23] Beyond the polemic, the exegetical principle is clear. Luther thought apocalyptic easily gets in the way of preaching Christ. That is not the conviction of the premillennialists. The religion of the book has become the empire of the savage text.

How, then, should these apocalyptic passages be interpreted? The first task is to challenge the assumptions on which the dangerous nonsense of millennialism is allowed to rest. For example, Matthew's Jesus speaks of "great tribulation," but this is no license whatever for thinking the Great Tribulation is an imminent event. Matthew almost certainly had in mind the conflagration in 68–70 CE when the city and temple of Jerusalem were destroyed. The Roman historian Josephus records that 1,100,000 people were killed during the siege, and a further 97,000 captured and enslaved.[24] That is certainly comparable to an event "such as was not since the beginning of the world to this time." If the thousand-year rule of Christ and the saints is interpreted figuratively, and not forced into some febrile chronology, the martyrs are the first to share in the final triumph of Christ over all empires. And that *is* the traditional teaching of the Church before biblicism was ever countenanced. (Known as "preterism." from the Latin *praeter*, "past," it is the assumption that many of the apocalyptic visions and utterances of both Testaments have already been fulfilled.)

The Roman Catholic Church endorses no version of millennialism. While the Catechism mentions the Antichrist, "he" is not a human being but "a pseudo-messianism by which man glorifies himself in place of God." That Church rejects "even modified forms of this falsification of the kingdom to come under the name of millenarianism [*sic*]."[25] The Orthodox churches of the East are similarly reluctant to literalize Christ's thousand-year reign. For them the number 1,000 is just an undesignated but immeasurable time. Christ rules now, through the Church, and his Kingdom or rule will be complete at his return. This represents the Christian hope, and does not need to be mapped onto passing historical events. The Nicene Creed (325 CE) contains the sentence: "And he shall come again with glory to judge both the quick and the dead, whose kingdom shall have no end." The final clause of this sentence was included to counteract any suggestion that the thousand years of Christ's rule meant literally that Christ would rule for a thousand years. The ancient churches, unaffected by the biblicism of the modern period, are exempted from the charge of reducing apocalyptic to the status of savage texts.

Nonetheless there is an important place for apocalyptic in contemporary Christianity which evades biblical literalism and imperial ideology. The entire genre has become strange to us, even though secular versions abound in science fiction, in a huge range of films such as *The Children of Men* (2006) and *The Day after Tomorrow* (2004), and pop songs such as REM's *It's the End of the World as We Know It (And I Feel Fine)* (1988). Star wars, space invaders, flying saucers, extraterrestrials, and the like are the secular successors of apocalyptic, all preying on the contrary senses of cosmic alarm and fascination with the unexpected and the unknown. The Gospel writers were heavily influenced by the events in the Roman province of Judea which culminated in the fall of Jerusalem and the destruction of the temple. Since these events took place in the middle of the period when the books of the New Testament were being written, it is not surprising that references to them are made. Relations between Christians and Jews were becoming worse in that decade as the new missionary faith became more detached from its Jewish roots (see chapter 6 below). The language and tone of cataclysm lay to hand, and found itself fulfilled in these horrors. The book of Revelation was written at a time of persecution of Christians and their churches, and its vision of the

Roman empire as an evil empire, whose overcoming at the hands of Almighty God was assured, provided encouragement to them. The book may be well read today as a prophecy of the ultimate doom of all empires which act unjustly, which persecute their opponents, and scorch the earth in pursuit of imperial gain.

As for the immediate future of planet earth, the extent of human responsibility for ozone depletion, species extinction, global warming, and so on, is becoming better known. So is the reduced room for urgent human remedial action in reducing the damage. Bad apocalyptic theology accepts no responsibility for the state of the planet, even though the deep ecological pessimism it engenders compounds the problem and has undoubtedly contributed to it. It was prophesied. God foreknew it and even brought it to pass. The state of the earth is instead God's own summons to individual repentance. Christian theology can do much better than this. The Gospels understand Jesus to have established the Reign or Kingdom of God. This is the realm of the power of God manifested in the healing of illness and disability, in caring for the sick, in the casting out of the power of demons to disrupt and destroy personal and political life, in rearranging relations of power to make them relations of justice, in rehabilitating society's outcasts, in feeding the hungry, in clothing the naked, and in countless other ways. This really *is* Gospel, the Good News of God's breaking into the natural and human worlds in order to remove the root causes of our alienation from each other and from God.

Everyone knows that such a reign is far from being accomplished and that the one who inaugurated it was crucified by the very powers he had non-violently opposed. His death, according to believers in every generation, is the self-enacted parable of the God who gives and goes on giving, and even gives Godself. Christ's resurrection is the vindication of Christ's self-sacrifice. It proclaims that his way of being-in-the-world is approved by God; that it is also God's way-of-being-in-the-world as suffering Love. Inasmuch as believers locate themselves within any ultimate time-frame, they live between two events. The first event is the coming of Jesus, the event wherein eternity breaks into time. It is *the* event which gives sense to time and to history.

The second event is the end of history, barely thinkable, yet bringing to completion the Reign of God that Jesus inaugurated, and which in early Christian preaching was called the "restitution of all things" (Acts 3:21). We live between these events and eagerly await the fulfillment of the Kingdom.

Above all, the Gospel is the enactment of hope in God. Hope is one of the great theological virtues (1 Corinthians 13:13). Temptations to despair are many, and they include many of the features of the world that are also the objects of apocalyptic imagination: famine, war, devastation, extra-terrestrial signs and events, extraordinary natural phenomena, and so on. The affluence of the Christian West and its corrosion of our souls, the ridiculous divisions within and between the different churches, the mutual hatreds and misunderstandings within and between the religions (even as they preach peace to the rest of us), and the rise of fundamentalisms proclaiming pseudo-certainty in the face of perplexity, and pseudo-simplicity in the face of complexity, are all temptations to despair. The savage texters of the Apocalypse give in to this temptation. The message of the premillennialists is that things can only get worse and worse, until the Rapture rescues the faithful who have read the apocalyptic runes in the same way that they do. Modern apocalyptic is much more dangerous than private misconstrual of scripture. It saps Christians of their staple need of hope, and when it is allied to the global ambitions of the empire of the United States and the remorseless logic of global capitalism, the danger of its pronouncements are all too plain.

Again we have found the savagery of the biblical text results from interpretations which fail to focus upon the central Christian doctrines of God and what God does in Christ. They are seduced by the ease of reading the Bible as God's independent and inspired Word. Thankfully a major authoritative commentary on the book of Revelation confirms that faith in Jesus must always take priority over faith in apocalyptic. Judith Kovacs and Christopher Rowland conclude: "The gospel stories constitute the framework for understanding what counts as faithfulness to Jesus. It is the memory of Jesus which is to be invoked, shared and wrestled with in the articulation of a contemporary faith." Their work follows the trajectory of this volume in claiming "Christian faith is given shape by the gospels, not by the epistles (or for that matter the Apocalypse). The rest of the New Testament bears witness to a creative exploration of what faith may mean in new situations that are removed from the particularity of Jesus' circumstances."[26] This is well said, and not only in relation to the Apocalypse. The memory of Jesus is pivotal to contemporary exploration of faith. Everything else in the two Testaments can assist in the renewed understanding of who he is and what he does. When we give similar credence to the texts of apocalypse as we give to the apocalypse, or revelation, of God-in-Christ, savagery is the normal outcome.

5

"Take Now Thy Son":
The Bible and Children

The basic contrast in this book (as readers will by now know!) is between God, the Word made flesh, and the Bible through which God's Word is known. Perhaps no subject illustrates the contrast between the teaching of Jesus, the very Word of God, and the teachings in the rest of the Bible, than children. There are two aims to this chapter. The first aim is to demonstrate that the Bible contains material about children which, in the hands of literal-minded Bible readers, becomes morally problematic and even dangerous to children. In order to draw this contrast it will be necessary to fix our eyes on more unpleasantness, in particular the narrative describing Abraham's willingness to sacrifice his son Isaac. The second aim is to insist that any follower of Jesus should, in the case of children, follow his child-affirming teaching and turn away from the child-averse teaching found elsewhere in the Bible. It will be shown that this can only be done if the basic contrast between God the Word and the Bible is reaffirmed, and the status of Jesus raised over against the Bible in Christian faith and devotion.

Jesus and Children

The teachings of Jesus about children are fairly familiar. They are unique in the scriptures and in the ancient world. Mark records "And they brought young children to him, that he should touch them: and his disciples rebuked those that brought them" (Mark 10:13).

This contrast between welcome and rebuke has been played out in every generation since the time of Jesus, and it haunts the churches even now.[1] For example, my church, the Church of England, has debated for 40 years whether baptized but yet-to-be-confirmed children are welcome at Holy Communion. During this time the number of children attending churches in England has precipitously declined. Synod has at last decided that they may now receive the bread and wine (subject to the diocesan bishop's absolute discretion).[2] Jesus teaches that the Reign of God belongs to children: "of such is the kingdom of God" (Mark 10:14). Children belong to the Reign of God just because, like the poor, the hungry, and the suffering, they are powerless and vulnerable.[3] Jesus says: "Whosoever shall not receive the kingdom of God as a little child, he shall not enter therein" (Mark 10:15). The term "childness" has been used to elucidate this saying. Childness[4] is a range of *human* qualities that children exemplify and adults are likely to compromise or lose. These qualities are, at least, "vulnerability, openness, immediacy, and neediness." Matthew records how, when his disciples asked Jesus "Who is the greatest in the kingdom of Heaven?," Jesus "called a little child unto him, and set him in the midst of them, and said, 'Verily I say unto you, Except ye be converted, and become as little children, ye shall not enter the kingdom of heaven'" (Matthew 18:1–3). Matthew's Jesus critiques the hierarchical and androcentric structures of households. The *human* quality of humility is specified again and again. Children have it and adults are in danger of losing it.[5]

"Whosoever shall receive one of such children in my name," said Jesus, "receiveth me: and whosoever shall receive me, receiveth not me, but him that sent me" (Mark 9:36–7). This saying challenges both what we take God to be and where God is manifested in the human world. There is an assumed solidarity of Jesus with children which is as theologically robust as his more familiar solidarity with God the Father (and with which theology is more comfortable).[6] Jesus teaches that for adults to inflict harm on children is a horrendous crime (Matthew 18:6–7). Children are shown to have an innate understanding of who Jesus is (Matthew 21:15–16). Even babies understand what the learned and wise do not (Matthew 11:25).

There can be little doubt that Jesus had a particular and intense love for children. How the atmosphere changes when we move into the rest of the New Testament! The author of Ephesians contrasts "the stature of the fullness of Christ" with the gullible state of childhood which Christians are to eschew (Ephesians 4:13–14). The author of 1 Timothy thinks that having children is how women make reparation for their collective responsibility for bringing wickedness into the world through the disobedience to God of the first woman, Eve (1 Timothy 2:15). In the New Testament "childbearing is if anything discouraged." This verse is "the one justification for it."[7] Paul's inspirational poem about the greatest of the Spirit's fruits, love, is less positive about the provisional and immature state of childhood: "When I was a child, I spake like a child, I understood as a child, I thought as a child: but when I became a man, I put away childish things" (1 Corinthians 13:11).

The discouragement of marriage in the New Testament and the warning against its attendant cares (including children?!) also strikes a dissonant chord. St. Paul's preference for celibacy (1 Corinthians 7:25–38) has been very influential, and for the first 1,500 years of Christendom so has the warning of Jesus that "The children of this world marry, and are given in marriage: But they which shall be accounted worthy to obtain that world, and the resurrection from the dead, neither marry, nor are given in marriage" (Luke 20:34–5). If celibacy is better than marriage then it is better not to have children than to have them. The Household Codes affirm a hierarchical order in the household, as in the Roman empire, and children are required to display unquestioning obedience to their parents (Ephesians 6:1; Colossians 3:20). Obedience is the precondition of the patriarchal order.

Children in the Old Testament

The Old Testament contains terrible calumnies against children. While children (and especially sons) are regarded as signs of God's blessing, the Hebrew scriptures (at least in conservative hands) also leave a sour, baleful, lingering influence on the contemporary understanding of childhood. Their justification for beating children has heavily influenced every century of Christianity, including the present one.

> He that spareth his rod hateth his son: but he that loveth him chasteneth him betimes. (Proverbs 13:24)
>
> Foolishness is bound in the heart of a child; but the rod of correction shall drive it far from him. (Proverbs 22:15)
>
> Withhold not correction from the child: for if thou beatest him with the rod, he shall not die. Thou shalt beat him with the rod, and shalt deliver his soul from hell. (Proverbs 23:13–14)[8]

These verses do not merely grant permission to beat children (or, as we rightly say, abuse them); they also castigate any reluctance to beat them as a failure of *love*. Beating is commanded here. It is a matter of life and death that it be regularly carried out. These ghastly ratiocinations (of the male mind) ignore the emotional and physical scars inflicted on infant and juvenile bodies. In Christian hands they have been thought to license the "breaking of a child's will" or the driving out of original sin, or (as in many Protestant homes today) the delusive infliction of "loving discipline," in the name of the Father God who authorizes it.

The author of Ecclesiasticus goes further. Imagine reading the following advice in a contemporary booklet for young, inexperienced parents:

> Pamper a boy and he will shock you;
> join in his games and he will grieve you.
> Do not share his laughter, or you will share his pain
> and end by grinding your teeth.
> While he is young do not give him freedom
> or overlook his errors.

> While he is young break him in,
> and beat him soundly while he is still a child;
> otherwise he may grow stubborn and disobedient
> and cause you distress. (Ecclesiasticus 30:9–12)[9]

Would not the author, and his publisher, be arrested today for such vicious sentiments? As John Spong observes (with reference to the child-beating passages in Proverbs), "If one is the *victim* of corporal punishment, these words suggest a sense of 'deserving' and thereby play into a self-negativity that rises from a particular definition of humanity. If one is the *perpetrator* of corporal punishment, these words seem to feed a human need to control, to exercise authority or even to demonstrate that forced submission is a virtue."[10] The highest value here, religious, familial, and moral, is (once more) obedience and submission – in other words, the patriarchal order is paramount, and even playing and laughing with children compromises it.

In another case of disobedience, the parents of an adolescent or young man are permitted to petition to have him killed! If he does not respond to corrective treatment,

> Then shall his father and his mother lay hold on him, and bring him out unto the elders of his city, and unto the gate of his place; and they shall say unto the elders of his city, This our son is stubborn and rebellious, he will not obey our voice; he is a glutton, and a drunkard. And all the men of his city shall stone him with stones, that he die: so shalt thou put evil away from among you; and all Israel shall hear, and fear. (Deuteronomy 21:19–21)

The son here is probably a young man (with access to alcohol?) living with his parents in the "House of the Father [*Beth-ab*]." Let us hope that this ultimate sanction was never invoked. But let us also distinguish between the teaching of Jesus about children and this cold affirmation of collective "power over." Let us contrast the teaching of Jesus son of

Sira (who wrote Ecclesiasticus) with the teaching of Jesus of Nazareth found in, say, the parable of the Prodigal Son (Luke 15:11–32), where a father is overjoyed at the return of a son who squandered his share of the family fortune and dragged the family name into disrepute. Why do so many Christians find it so difficult to repudiate this pre-Christian, sub-Christian, or even anti-Christian material when they have the teaching and example of Jesus to follow? Because it is in the Bible, the Church's guidebook? Scripture "teaches" it, even if we must pretend that it doesn't. But not all Christians *do* pretend that it doesn't.

At other times the death of large numbers of children seems to function in order to embellish a narrative without any indication that the author values their loss. The prophet Elisha did not like children teasing him on account of his baldness, so he "looked on them, and cursed them in the name of the Lord. And there came forth two she bears out of the wood, and tare forty and two children of them" (2 Kings 2:24). God apparently is more concerned with protecting the fragile dignity of his prophet from the gentle teasing of playful children than he is in sparing them from death and terrible injury. Elisha is not the only prophet whose arrival is bad news for real children. The birth of Moses takes place after Pharaoh's edict to his people that "every [Hebrew] son that is born ye shall cast into the river" (Exodus 1:22). When God delivered the Israelites from slavery in Egypt, was there really an inscrutable holy need for the Lord to smite "all the firstborn in the land of Egypt, from the firstborn of Pharaoh that sat on his throne unto the firstborn of the captive that was in the dungeon; and all the firstborn of cattle" (Exodus 12:29)? When Matthew depicts the birth of Jesus as the birth of the new Moses, he too inserts a massacre of young children in order to make his theological point. "Herod … was exceeding wroth, and sent forth, and slew all the children that were in Bethlehem, and in all the coasts thereof, from two years old and under" (Matthew 2:16). The arrival of the Messiah was good news for the world, but it wasn't good news for those particular children. We do not need to understand what is called "the massacre of the innocents" as a historical event (or indeed the story of the slaughter of the Israelite children either). They may be no more than background

83

details in adult stories which convey deep theological meanings. In Matthew's Gospel Jesus is the new Moses. If the stage setting of Act 1 (Moses) in the two-act drama of salvation required the death of every newly born male child, the stage setting of Act 2 (Jesus) requires similar, recognizable, detail in order to emphasize that at Bethlehem One greater than Moses was born. But the literalizing mindset is unhappy that these ghastly stories might not be literally true. And there is an obvious consequence. God kills children. Or God lets them die. When God sends or protects God's prophets, children die. Even when God the Son comes as a baby, there is more pointless child-killing.

The Sacrifice of Isaac

Sadly, we have now arrived at perhaps the ghastliest point in all scripture and biblical history, the sacrifice of children, and the modeling of the sacrifice of Jesus on the cross as the supreme instance of child sacrifice. I suspect we Christians will make little progress in honoring children, and the teaching of Jesus about them, unless and until we acknowledge the harm done to our tradition by the shadow cast on children by the story of Abraham's willingness to sacrifice his child Isaac.[11] We also need to own its lingering influence upon the treatment of children and young people in Christian cultures right down to the present. This, however, will be difficult to achieve, since it is a founding narrative of the faith. The story, called the **Akedah** (Genesis 22:1–18) may require a stiff drink just to get through it. God tests Abraham's obedience by telling him to *kill* his son Isaac:

> Take now thy son, thine only son Isaac, whom thou lovest, and get thee into the land of Moriah; and offer him there for a burnt offering upon one of the mountains which I will tell thee of. (Genesis 22:2)

Abraham does as he is told. He "built an altar ... and laid the wood in order, and bound Isaac his son, and laid him on the altar upon the wood. And Abraham stretched forth his hand, and took the knife to slay his son" (Genesis 22:9–10). An angel intervenes. Abraham's obedience is first amply verified, then amply rewarded. A ram "caught in a thicket by his horns" (22:13) is killed instead. The Lord is delighted that Abraham is willing to kill his own child. The reward for such extreme obedience is the blessing of the nations. "And in thy seed shall the nations of the earth be blessed; because thou hast obeyed my voice" (22:18). Willingness to kill a child is the indispensable premise on which the salvation of the nations depends. The implication is unmistakable. We who are saved are saved because Abraham was prepared to stick a knife in his own child's throat.

This story bristles with historical, moral, and theological difficulties. Even more depressing and sinister is its constant reception in Judaism, Christianity, and Islam (where it is hugely influential). Søren Kierkegaard's (1813–55) interpretation of the story is influential in modern Western thought. It filled him, he said, with repulsion and dread,[12] but his visceral reaction to it was the realization that "knights of faith" *are* required to demonstrate their willingness to make sacrifices of just this appalling kind.[13] The issues are vast, so we need to confine ourselves to a brief treatment of two questions pertinent to the theme of this chapter: did the God of Israel really demand the sacrifice of children? And how has the story impacted upon the sociocultural and religious understandings of the character of God and the disposability of children? Children are, of course, highly valued among Jewish people past and present. They are proof of fertility, and the hope of protection in old age and extension of the line of kinship. Yet the very value accorded to them makes them ideal candidates for the ultimate religious loyalty test. How does a man prove that he loves God more than anyone or anything else? The answer is horrifyingly clear.

Yes, the God of Israel *did* require child sacrifice. However, the issue is not straightforward, and since all non-psychopathic Christians have an interest in denying it, it is important to discuss the evidence carefully. Part of the evidence is the narrative just discussed. Jon Levenson has assembled more. He takes literally the commandment "the firstborn of thy sons shalt thou give unto me" (Exodus 22:28).[14] Not every father practiced it. The substitution of an animal was allowed, thereby "redeeming the child," but "animal sacrifice did not, in this situation, *replace* child sacrifice. Rather, the animal *substituted* for the child: the god's claim upon the youngster was realized through the death of the nonhuman stand-in."[15] A clear case of human sacrifice is Jephthah's immolation of his own daughter (Judges 11:29–40). This warrior makes a bargain with the Lord: if he beats the Ammonites in battle, "then it shall be, that whatsoever cometh forth of the doors of my house to meet me, when I return in peace from the children of Ammon, shall surely be the Lord's, and I will offer it up for a burnt offering" (11:31). Unfortunately his only daughter (unnamed) "came out to meet him with timbrels and with dances" (11:34). No matter how rash the vow, her father "did with her according to his vow which he had vowed" (11:39). Jephthah regrets the vow, but there is nothing in the narrative to suggest that this was an unworthy sacrifice, or that the Lord was displeased with either the vow or the ritual murder of a young, innocent woman.

Deniers of child murder in the Lord's name have no way of tinkering with the clarity of this sickening narrative. The most they can do is attempt to confine the practice to this single instance. Less straightforwardly there are several other Old Testament passages which suggest the continuity of the practice. An incident in 2 Kings 3 describes what Mesha, king of Moab did, when he realized he was losing the war with the Israelites. "Then he took his eldest son that should have reigned in his stead, and offered him for a burnt offering upon the wall. And there was great indignation against Israel: and they departed from him, and returned to their own land" (3:27). There is an obvious objection to this story being used as evidence for child sacrifice within Israel. Mesha was king of *Moab*. But there is a counter-objection. "Mesha's sacrifice worked. By immolating his first-born son and heir apparent, the king of Moab was able to turn the tide of battle and force the Israelites to retreat." It follows, thinks Levenson, that the author of 2 Kings acknowledged "the full acceptability of this act."[16] The practice of child sacrifice is thought to be directly addressed by the prophet Micah when he asks, "Shall I give my firstborn for my transgression, the fruit of my body for the sin of my soul?" (Micah 6:7). Why is the practice questioned if it was not done? That question must also be asked of the prophet Jeremiah's condemnation of it. Judgment is coming *upon the Israelites* because "They have built also the high places of Baal, to burn their sons with fire for burnt offerings unto Baal, which I commanded not, nor spake it, neither came it into my mind" (Jeremiah 19:5–6, and see 7:31).

Elsewhere, where Jeremiah condemns the Israelites for causing "their sons and their daughters to pass through the fire unto Molech" (32:35), an apparent foreign deity is blamed for the practice. So Jeremiah repudiates and proscribes the sacrifice of children. He says it has no part in Israel's origins and founding texts. But that is because he speaks at a later time when the moral revulsion against the practice was beginning to become mainstream. Why condemn it if it was not going on? If it was never commanded, what are we to make of Abraham's obedience?

The prophet Ezekiel has a different take on child sacrifice. It is God's fault for giving the Israelites bad laws. Ezekiel has God say: "I also gave them over to statutes that were not good and laws they could not live by; I let them become defiled through their gifts – the sacrifice of every firstborn – that I might fill them with horror so they would know that I am the LORD" (Ezekiel 20:25–6[17]).

So there are two competing explanations for the practice, each in tension with the other. In one it is not part of Israel's origins but involves sacrificing to another god. But there was no such god. Rather the term *mlk* (anglicized as Molech or Molek) is associated with the sacrifices of children and lambs in the world around Israel.[18] In the other, God (incredibly) commands the sacrifice of firstborn children in order to bring about the devastation of God's own people.[19] Ezekiel's God is certainly responsible for everything that happens, including the evil of child sacrifice, but the "horror" instilled in a generation of readers influenced by critical study of the Bible must surely be disavowal, and repudiation. In the name of Jesus Christ this God needs to be removed from the moral and religious consciousness of such humanity.

While the existence of child sacrifice therefore seems incontrovertible, there are also scholars who deny it ever occurred. One of these is Carol Delaney (who, as we shall shortly see, is sharply critical of the assumptions behind the story of the *Akedah* narrative). If the *Akedah* narrative is just that, a narrative, it need not be taken as evidence that child sacrifice occurred either in the time of Abraham or subsequently. If the practice is assumed, then several biblical references are interpreted as if that assumption were historically verifiable, but it is not.[20] The historical argument is far from over. My colleague at Exeter, Francesca Stavrakopoulou, at the end of a long and convincing study, concludes: "Child sacrifice appears to have been a native and normative element of Judahite religious practice." In many places, she says, "it would appear that the biblical writers have intentionally distorted their presentation of child sacrifice in an attempt to distance their ancestors and their god YHWH from a practice which came to be rejected within certain post-monarchic circles."[21] I have admitted there is an argument going on (which must be left to the historians, the Hebraists, the archaeologists, and scholars of the ancient Near East). Clearly there is for Jews and Christians a *preferred* interpretation: it never happened. There is no moral problem at all.

That is the attitude taken by scores of Protestant theologians who appear to ignore the moral enormity of what they read. Consider, for example, David Ford's oblivious treatment of the passage in *Christian Wisdom*. He describes the incident without a flicker of recognition of its moral ambivalence, and then leaps, with dubious innocence, to its import for today's Christians seeking a "wisdom interpretation of scripture." The story teaches them that "The practical implication of fearing God is the conformity of one's life to God, even if that means dying. *God is more important than life itself, whether one's own life or that of those who may be dearer than one's own life.*"[22] This treatment of the story leaves its primitive, morally repugnant features intact. It juxtaposes the love of God and the love of children in a tragic quasi-dilemma. Why persist with these unwholesome dichotomies? What God worthy of worship would expect us to kill our children in some shabby, macho loyalty test? Is that the devotion God wants? Is it really Christian wisdom to assume God's love plunges us into these mind-numbing extremities of devotion? For the sake of God's revelation in Christ, it is more appropriate to bind and burn the concept of God that the story assumes than it is to attempt to draw cozy lessons from it.

The standard method of dealing with the *Akedah* text is to claim, as Christians and Jews generally do, that God does not permit child sacrifice (how could "he"?): indeed the provision of the ram indicates that only animal sacrifice is acceptable. The narrative is evidence instead of its prohibition. If there once was the abominable practice of the sacrifice of the firstborn, then this story marks its final cessation. But this rationalization of the plain evil of the text no longer holds water. As Delaney (who, as we have seen, is skeptical about the histo-ricity of the practice) says, "even if child sacrifice was practiced in the ancient Near East … such interpretations fail to recognize that Abraham is revered not for putting an end to the practice but for his willingness to go through with it. *That* is what establishes him as the father of faith. *That* is what I find so terrifying."[23] Levenson, who is in no doubt about the practice, agrees. On the assumption that the *Akedah* narrative signals the substitution of animal for human sacrifice, he notes "That those making the assumption share a proper horror for human sacrifice further discourages them from scrutinizing the anal-ogy more carefully, lest it come to appear that this treasured text, of such eminent centrality to both Judaism and Christianity, actually accepts something that the normative teachings of both those tradi-tions condemn categorically."[24] I have found understandable resist-ance from Christian audiences when I have sought to create respectable moral distance between the teaching of the Son of God about chil-dren and the ancient God who sometimes requires their ritual murder. Abraham is rewarded precisely because of his willingness to kill his child, not for killing a substitutionary ram. His willingness to do this is as central to the story as it is unpalatable. Delaney asks, "if he was willing, how does that make him different from, or better than, his neighbours who, supposedly, were also willing, and did go through with the sacrifice?" It is his willingness to do it that makes him Father of Faith, not the fact that God put an end to the practice. And God blessed him because he did not withhold his son (Gen 22:16–18). If the story was meant as a prohibition or modification of the practice of human sacrifice, God could have said as much, or the biblical authors could have represented him making such an injunction.[25]

The story "celebrates the type of consciousness that wants to be commanded to perform extreme acts of obedience by an absolute authority whose attractiveness lies in its very refusal to explain itself." Its power "lies in the unthinking nature of the obedience that is demanded."[26] There is much more in the story requiring challenge. What did Isaac's mother Sarah think about all this (assuming she knew)?[27] How badly was Isaac permanently damaged by his horrifying ordeal?[28] To what extent is the story about the male power to create life through the male "seed" and therefore also to dispose of it?[29] I shall move instead to the deeper problem for Christians: the possible impact of the *Akedah* on Christian civilization, especially the sacrifice of young men in unnecessary wars. Child sacrifice, says Stavrakopoulou, has an "afterlife." It lives on in other forms. Male circumcision within Judaism may be one such form. But there are others. "Another long-lasting 'afterlife' of child sacrifice may also be perceived in the continuing Christian designation of Jesus as the 'only-begotten', 'beloved' and 'firstborn' son of God, sacrificed as a Passover lamb."[30] Isaac is Abraham's "only son … whom thou lovest" (Genesis 22:2; see also verses 12, 16). Jephthah's daughter "was his only child; beside her he had neither son nor daughter" (Judges 11:34). The parallelism between these and New Testament verses describing Jesus as the only begotten, beloved Son, "given" for us (for example, John 3:16) is unmistakable. We cannot deviate into the area of theology called **substitutionary atonement** which tries to have it that the just God justly punishes God's Son (who is also fully God) for something the Son didn't do in any case (commit sin).[31] We will confine ourselves instead to the possible impact of the story on attitudes to children and young people within Christendom. Delaney shockingly contends that the afterlife of the story extends far beyond biblical times; *that it has been internalized and assimilated so completely that the need for the sacrifice of young men in war has become ideologically legitimized in all the faiths the story influences*:

> This story, at the foundation of the three monotheistic religions, has shaped the social, cultural, and moral climates of the societies animated by them. It provides the supreme model of faith, and it incorporates notions of procreation, paternity, the family, gender definitions and roles, authority, and obedience. It is a symbolic representation of patriarchal power, and the structure, roles, and values that support it. Once these ideas, structures, and values have been internalized psychologically, rationalized philosophically, codified legally, and embedded in institutions such as marriage and the family, the military, and the church, they become part of the reality we live.[32]

This is clearly a huge and very damaging claim that requires careful evaluation. Let us consider it alongside two further repugnant claims, the first of which is made by Michael Northcott (whose analysis of millennialism was considered in the previous chapter). He argues that biblical religion sanctifies the violent deaths of hundreds of thousands of young Americans in wars waged by "the American Empire."[33] The argument does not mention the *Akedah* specifically, and in order to remain focused on children I am extending that category to include adolescents and young people, the people in fact who bear the brunt of sacrifice in war.

In summary form the argument is this: (1) All empires require the sacrifice of soldiers in order to defend their territory and interests. (2) Empires produce cults which provide religious or sacral reinforcement of these deaths. (3) In the USA, "civil religion" provides this reinforcement. Civil religion sacralizes imperial interests, particularly through the veneration of the national flag and the totemic significance it is accorded. (4) In the American case civil religion draws on a form of Protestant fundamentalism. This kind of Protestantism privatizes and individualizes faith, that is, it evacuates faith from the public world, thereby rendering prophetic criticism of public policy superfluous, and confines itself to the inner life of souls and their vertical relationship to God. (5) Now for the sting in the argument. In order to reinforce the interests of the empire, sacrifices must be seen to be *costly*. Recognition of this crucial need for costliness, especially when the causes for which sacrifice is demanded are contentious, yields the conclusion (6) "that it is the violent death of *Americans* and not of America's enemies which is the true sacrifice that is effective in uniting the nation around its totem flag."[34] This would explain why "America has always been prepared to commit so many of its people, and so much of its resources, to the military, and to weapons that kill." In the Vietnam, Korean, and Gulf wars, "America had more than 110,000 war dead, and 250,000 wounded. None of the wars involved any threat to the territorial integrity of the United States. But they served a larger purpose, in advancing the [civil] religion of America."[35] All this without a mention of the unimaginable war in Iraq.

The link between the analyses of Northcott and Delaney lies in the social willingness to sacrifice young men either because God commands it, or because some other authority does. *Dulce et decorum est pro patria mori*.[36] The model of faith in the *Akedah* "implies that to be faithful, fathers ought to be willing to sacrifice their sons if God, or some other transcendent authority, such as the State demands ... The faithful *man* is a man whose faith in an abstract, transcendent concept (God) takes precedence over his earthly, emotional tie to his child; his faith renders him invulnerable to human claims."[37]

The second claim is based on the impact of the *Akedah* narrative on particular individuals. Delaney's work begins with an account of a father on trial in California for murdering his child because God had told him to do so through the *Akedah* story.[38] A chaplain at a mental health hospital tells me of a patient who tried to sacrifice his son and another who had murdered his wife because she was disobedient. Both utilize the Bible to justify their actions. She warns against the "danger of God being depicted in terms of the supreme psychopath," and observes that "those who suffer from personality disorder (psychopaths) always need to feel in control of situations and other people. They become adept at controlling others and when they do not get their own way they can quickly become angry."[39] These are extreme cases, yet extreme cases of cruelty to children are far more common than we probably want to think.[40]

Putting Jesus First

Delaney does not claim that the *Akedah* narrative is solely responsible for the sacrifice of sons, or for the propensity towards violence by individuals or states. "It is not enough to point to *concomitance*: one must show that religion is a *salient* cause of the deplored effects."[41] Her claim is more that the narrative is a classic text of patriarchy, with its power over life and death, its assumption about the disposability of children, and much else. I take it to be a thick strand, which with others, constitutes the rope of violence that still binds many believers within the Semitic faiths to an angry, patriarchal, capricious god. In the end it is easier to believe in such a god, for the conviction that "he" exists effectively prevents our transformation into the compassionate people we are to become if we are to be followers of Christ.

Northcott's explanation for violence within the American empire may likewise fall short of demonstrating that religion is a *salient* cause of the deplored effects. But it is doubtful whether any relationship of cause and effect can be established within the realm of ideas or large-scale explanations. In the meantime we have to make do with imaginative connections, plausibilities, degrees of explanatory power, and so on. Even if the probability that he is right is relatively low, his analysis ought to compel a reappraisal of American millennialism and fundamentalism. The impact of biblical narratives upon psychopathically inclined individuals who murder their kin may also not get much further than ***post hoc* rationalizations** of actions already undertaken. But that does not acquit Bible users and readers from the charge of dangerous, even murderous, interpretations of their holy book. We have already noted the disingenuity of Christians condemning homophobic prejudice while pretending that some of their current attitudes, beliefs, and doctrines do not continue to contribute directly to it. A similar situation arises here. There are dangerous biblical texts where children do not fare well. Even the possibility that their afterlife lingers on anywhere among Christian people, helping to produce "a continuous substrate of moral consciousness for millennia"[42] should compel a renewed heart-searching among the churches.

The teaching of Jesus with which the chapter began is uncompromising in its respect and love for children. The problems that have been allowed to arise in this chapter are the consequence of placing other biblical teaching about children on the same level of importance as the teaching of Jesus within a typical "Word of God framework." When this is done in the name of excessive regard for the literal meanings of biblical passages, that teaching of Jesus is inevitably compromised and loses its child-devoted originality and richness.[43] Once the Word of God in flesh has been separated out from the words of scripture, and the latter allowed to witness to the former, not least by pointing to our need for deliverance from violence, the compulsion to find God speaking today in these terrible texts disappears and the voice of Jesus is heard with a renewed and sonorous clarity.

6

"Thou Shalt Not Suffer a Witch to Live": The Bible, Jews, and Women

There have been many similarities in the case studies we have so far considered. The written text of the Bible has been used against minorities: against same-sex couples, black people, slaves, non-Christians, victims of violence, and children. Imperial power and its practices have been legitimized by the churches and their theologians on the basis of what the Bible allegedly says. Biblical texts are identified and utilized as grounds for exercising power over powerless groups of people. A clue to the ideological use of the Bible in these cases is the implausibility of the interpretation offered. In each case, there are similar assumptions about what the Bible is for. It is used to "speak" authoritatively on all kinds of issues independently of the Word of God made flesh in Christ. These interpretations, thankfully, have not always prevailed, not least because other Christians have successfully posed counter-arguments.

The present chapter presents two further case studies in biblical bullying, albeit more briefly. By now the die is cast, the pattern established. However, the issues are not minor; indeed, they are arguably as lethal to human flourishing as any so far considered. Brevity of treatment here must not be the measure of actual misery caused. The Bible has been used against Jews in appalling Christian anti-Semitism, and against women, in a holy misogyny that still remains lodged in the exclusive ordination practices of most of Christendom. These cases conclude the case studies in biblical interpretation which are the subject of part II.

The Bible and Anti-Semitism

The treatment of Jews by Christians over 20 centuries exceeds in violence the treatment of Christians by Christians in the European wars of the early modern period. The biblical sources of hatred are, in this instance, even less comforting for contemporary Christians because they are found in the very Gospel records themselves.

The parable of the Wicked Husbandmen records how the owner of a vineyard lets it to tenants, and emigrates. He sends his servants at different times to collect some fruit, and the tenants wound or kill each of them:

> Having yet therefore one son, his wellbeloved, he sent him also last unto them, saying, They will reverence my son. But those husbandmen said among themselves, This is the heir; come, let us kill him, and the inheritance shall be our's. And they took him, and killed him, and cast him out of the vineyard. What shall therefore the lord of the vineyard do? he will come and destroy the husbandmen, and will give the vineyard unto others. (Mark 12:6–9)

The text (which refers closely to Isaiah 5:1–7) has an unmistakable implication: the Jews have murdered the Son of God. God will therefore murder them, and give their entire inheritance to "others," that is, to Christians. Which Jews? Mark is clear that he has their religious leaders in mind, "the chief priests, and the scribes, and the elders" (11:27, 12:12). The rest of the Jewish people "are depicted in positive terms."[1] Matthew and Luke also include this parable, but the changes they make show "they are increasingly concerned to interpret the death of Jesus in anti-Jewish terms."[2]

The Passion narratives of all four Gospels depict the Jews as responsible for the death of Jesus. Mark records how Pilate preferred to have Jesus released. But this time "the chief priests moved the people" (15:11) so that they, and not just their leaders, are incriminated. Matthew again adds to Mark's story. Pilate remonstrates unsuccessfully with the "multitude" and capitulates to their wishes:

> When Pilate saw that he could prevail nothing, but that rather a tumult was made, he took water, and washed his hands before the multitude, saying, I am innocent of the blood of this just person: see ye to it. Then answered all the people, and said, His blood be on us, and on our children. Then released he Barabbas unto them: and when he had scourged Jesus, he delivered him to be crucified. (Matthew 27:24–6)

Matthew's Gospel compounds the guilt of the Jews for the unjust execution of Jesus. Judas Iscariot confesses his guilt at having "betrayed the innocent blood" (27:4). Pilate's wife has a dream and tries to warn her husband against becoming involved. "A Roman woman becomes witness to Jesus' innocence, whereas the Jewish people, spurred on by the authorities, calls for Jesus' death."[3] The Roman governor indulges in a Jewish ritual act (publicly washing his hands), exculpating himself from the sentence he is to pronounce. Matthew chooses a solemn Old Testament formula by which the Jews condemn themselves – "His blood be on us."[4] The Jewish people, "all the people," curse themselves, and their children. "None of the anti-Jewish statements in the New Testament has provoked so much murder, misery and despair among Jews in subsequent church history as this."[5] This savage text wins first prize for its misery-inducing consequences.

Luke and John in their different ways also make the Jews responsible for Christ's death. In John the Jews have "the devil" as their "father," who "was a murderer from the beginning" (8:44). The early sermons recorded in Acts accuse the "men of Israel" of having crucified Jesus.[6] Paul accuses "the Jews" of having "killed the Lord Jesus, and their own prophets" (1 Thessalonians 2:15). Eusebius (c.265–340 CE), the church historian, records that God miraculously warned the Jerusalem Christians to evacuate the city before destroying it: "as if the royal city of the Jews and the whole land of Judea were entirely destitute of holy men, the judgement of God at length overtook those who had committed such outrages against Christ and his apostles, and totally destroyed that generation of impious men." Three million people died, estimated Eusebius (inaccurately), due to the addition of pilgrims in Jerusalem for Passover. He wished to assure his readers "that God was not long in executing vengeance upon them [the Jewish people] for their wickedness against the Christ of God."[7]

Luther's work *On the Jews and their Lies* can scarcely be mentioned, still less read, without a deep sense of shamed amazement. Is Christianity really capable of this? It is hard to find on Christian websites. On secular ones it is rightly preceded by a warning about its notoriety.[8] Luther's rant against them has a long prehistory. Their admitted sufferings and misfortunes since the fall of Jerusalem are due, he thinks, not to the persecution of Christians, but to the wrath of God upon them for their treatment of their Messiah, Jesus. Their failure to realize the true reason for their punishment testifies to their lack of intelligence and their spiritual blindness, and this renders discussion with them pointless. He quotes Hosea 1:9 against them ("for ye are not my people, and I will not be your God") to prove that they have forfeited any claim to be God's chosen people. This verse, and many others, become savage texts culminating in the "sincere advice" to "set fire to their synagogues or schools and to bury and cover with dirt whatever will not burn, so that no man will ever again see a stone or cinder of them."[9] Deuteronomy 13:16, and similar texts, are adduced to support destruction by fire as God's punishment for idolatry. Their houses should also be razed to the ground. They should live in barns like gypsies. All their prayer books and sacred texts should be taken from them, and rabbis not permitted to teach. Safe conduct for Jews on all public highways is to be withdrawn. They should not be allowed to lend money. All their silver and gold should be taken from them "for safe keeping," and to reward financially sincere individual converts to Christianity. All of them should be required to undertake forced labor. All this "is to be done," he continues, "in honour of our Lord and of Christendom, so that God might see that we are Christians, and do not condone or knowingly tolerate such public lying, cursing, and blaspheming of his Son and of his Christians." It is not difficult to surmise that Luther prepared the way for Adolf Hitler, and that the policies leading to the greatest crime of genocide Europe has known were strongly influenced by the shadow side of the Christian tradition that even now may not have run its course.

Once again it is the *critical* historical study of the Bible that eases Christian discomfort in the face of this appalling legacy. Jesus, the disciples, and the first Christians were Jews. The earliest records assume the Jewish *leaders*, not the Jewish people, wanted Jesus killed. The Romans killed Jesus: the crucifixion was a Roman method of execution. The early Christians remained "daily with one accord in the temple" (Acts 2:46). The Christian movement began as a movement within Judaism. Among these Jews, some believed that Jesus was the Christ, the Anointed One, the Messiah, whose coming was foretold in the Hebrew scriptures: some did not. As non-Jews joined the Christian movement, the tension within Jewish communities, between those who believed Jesus was the Messiah and those who did not, became acute. Jewish Christians began to be expelled from the synagogues, or to form their own churches.

The Gospels are written during the period of this heightened tension. The destruction of the Jerusalem temple by the Roman armies in 70 CE, was a terrible disaster for the Jewish people. As more and more Gentiles joined the (originally) Jewish Christians, the fledgling Christian faith drew, and grew, apart, and interpreted the fall of Jerusalem as God's judgment upon those Jews who did not believe the Christian Gospel. Matthew's and John's Gospels reflect the acrimony between the different groups of Christian and non-Christian Jews. The first great Church Council, in Jerusalem around 50 CE, was called in an attempt to settle the matter (see Acts 15:1–31; Galatians 2). Groups *within* Judaism often disputed furiously with one another about various questions. Their dispute with Christians began as one more such dispute. Paul, himself a Jew, outlined a mature model for thinking about the relationship between Jews and Christians. God's election of the Jews, he taught, was not cancelled by the incorporation of Gentiles into that unique relationship with God. Rather, it deserved honor, just because it existed before the Messiah had come (Romans 9–11; and see chapter 8 below). John's Gospel directly addresses (there are four references)[10] the excommunication of believing Jews (Christians) from the synagogue. Matthew was a Jewish Christian whose community had probably recently become detached from the synagogues. Nonetheless its remaining Jewishness may be seen from its conformity to the Law.[11] Most Christians just could not envisage any kind of historical future for an independent Judaism that refused to acknowledge the Jewish Messiah whom God had sent. None of the Gospel writers expected their Gospels to be collected up, preserved, formed into a canon, and made into a single guidebook with fixed, eternal meanings. They would be dismayed beyond measure to learn of the savagery they unwittingly sponsored and encouraged.

The Bible and Misogyny

> Thou shalt not suffer a witch to live. (Exodus 22:18)
>
> There shall not be found among you any one that maketh his son or his daughter to pass through the fire, or that useth divination, or an observer of times, or an enchanter, or a witch. Or a charmer, or a consulter with familiar spirits, or a wizard, or a necromancer. (Deuteronomy 18:10–11)

I have described a little of how in the hands of Luther the whole Bible became a savage text in relation to Jews. Just over half a century before the publication of *On The Jews and their Lies*, another noxious Christian work, the *Malleus Maleficarum* or *Hammer of Witches* (1486) contributed directly to the torture and death of many thousands of innocent women on the grounds that they were witches. This work defined witchcraft meticulously, using scripture, tradition, and reason eruditely. The authors were sincere practical theologians, authorized and affirmed by a **Papal Bull**. It justified the slaughter of witches (and "wizards") on biblical grounds, and prescribed in detail how witchcraft trials were to be conducted. Catholics and Protestants, bitterly divided in the following century, remained agreed that witches existed and had to be killed. In Scotland alone, a small, under-populated country, the Protestant Kirk ensured the death of over a thousand victims between 1590 and 1670 (not counting hundreds more who killed themselves or died awaiting trial). Between 1400 and 1800 between 40,000 and 50,000 people were executed for witchcraft in Europe and colonial North America.[12] The *Malleus* is one of the most destructive religious texts ever to be written. Readers need determination, and strong stomachs, to get through it. In its pages the Bible is converted into a savage text that vindicates misogyny and murder.

It must be understood that belief in the spirit world was rife in the fifteenth century, that illnesses were often causally attributed to the actions of devils, or their agents, witches. The practice of magic, beneficial and malevolent, was widespread. Beneficial magic might be used in the attempt, say, to heal a person or an animal from a sickness ("charming"). Maxwell-Stuart gives, as examples of malevolent magic, the laying of an illness on another person, the depriving of cows or human nursing mothers of milk, ruining a brewer's brew, using "the evil eye," and so on. He explains:

> the readiness with which Satan takes physical form in the psychology of this period ... the near-universal acceptance that the spiritual and material worlds were capable of interpenetration so frequent as to be almost constant, means that people who said they saw and heard and touched the Devil were experiencing certain moments in their lives in a way quite different from any which might occur to us ... These experiences of theirs were real in their terms.[13]

However, just at the time when these beliefs began to be seen as superstitious throughout Europe, the *Malleus* reinforced the supposed objective reality of witches and the misogyny that fed this belief. Witches exist. "Witch" constitutes a stable category of being. Witches feature in the Bible. Divine law requires they are to be put to death.[14] Since they deserve the death penalty, their crimes must be great. God permits the Devil to use them as God's agents. They must be tortured both in order to extract confession and exact just punishment. Early in the work the authors set themselves a prior question: "why a greater number of witches is found in the fragile feminine sex than among men."

The answer to that question is provided by an astonishing outburst of misogyny. Our interest in this must be confined to the authors' use of well-known passages of scripture, to their using these as savage texts, all in a very small section "Concerning Witches who copulate with Devils."[15] There is a rhetorical setting within which the misogyny is carefully placed. Women are also to be praised. Hers is the "sex in which God has always taken great glory." Women "know no moderation in goodness or vice." They can be exceptionally good and exceptionally wicked. Judith, Deborah, and Esther are examples of praiseworthy women. A believing woman is capable of sanctifying her unbelieving husband (1 Corinthians 7:14). "Blessed is the man who has a virtuous wife, for the number of his days shall be doubled" (Ecclesiasticus 26:1). Women have contributed to the spread of the Catholic faith. They are to be understood through "the benediction of MARY." "Therefore preachers should always say as much praise of them as possible."

We might call this type of writing "the apparatus of balance." That is, the contrived achievement of equanimity and impartiality serves as a pretext for launching outrageous accusations against people while maintaining the appearance of steadied neutrality. We have met the apparatus of balance before. It soon turns out that there is actually little to say in praise of women, the benediction of Mary notwithstanding, and much to say about their exceptional wickedness. The authors exploit the misogyny of Ecclesiasticus (or Sirach) 25: "There is no head above the head of a serpent: and there is no wrath above the wrath of a woman. I had rather dwell with a lion and a dragon than to keep house with a wicked woman"[16] (25:15–16); "All wickedness is but little to the wickedness of a woman" (25:19).[17]

The authors note that members of this "fragile, feminine sex" actually want to know why they are capable of such wickedness. Well, they are "more credulous," and "since the chief aim of the devil is to corrupt faith, therefore he rather attacks them." They are "more impressionable," and so "more ready to receive the influence of a disembodied spirit." And they have "slippery tongues" which render them "unable to conceal from their fellow-women those things which by evil arts they know."[18] These character deficits are all thought to be verified by the text of Ecclesiasticus 25. "As a jewel of gold in a swine's snout, so is a fair woman which is without discretion" (Proverbs 11:22).

With regard to the intellect, and to "the understanding of spiritual things," women "seem to be of a different nature from men." "Various examples from the Scriptures" confirm this. They are "intellectually like children." There is a decisive "natural reason" why women are as they are and why most consorters with evil spirits are women: "she is more carnal than a man, as is clear from her many carnal abominations." The authors rely on clearly specious interpretations of the Genesis account of the creation of Eve in order to show that, *even before the* **Fall**, the first woman was created imperfect, deceiving, doubting, and weak. The detail that God, while Adam was deeply asleep, "took one of his ribs" (Genesis 2:21) in order to make a woman, is made to support the further belief that the first woman "was formed from a bent rib, that is, a rib of the breast, which is bent as it were in a contrary direction." The conclusion from this unfortunate, but apparently divine, mistake is: "through this defect she is an imperfect animal, she always deceives." Samson's wife deceived him by her tears (Judges 14 – never mind that she was being blackmailed, by men [14:15]). Her example shows that *all* women are by nature deceitful.

Another *minutia* from Genesis 2 compounds the defect. The Lord God forbids the first couple to eat the fruit of "the tree of the knowledge of good and evil." They are told "for in the day that thou eatest thereof thou shalt surely die" (Genesis 2:17). The woman at first refuses the serpent's temptation to eat this fruit, citing the words of God: "God hath said, Ye shall not eat of it, neither shall ye touch it, lest ye die" (Genesis 3:3). The authors of the *Malleus* ignore that Eve quotes the words of God in her reply. No, her reply "lest ye die" somehow "showed that she doubted, and had little faith in the word of God"! That a woman is a natural doubter is then confirmed by the derivation of the Latin *femina*. It comes from *fe* and *minus*. *Minus* means in Latin roughly what it means in English, a lack. And that is why womankind is "ever weaker to hold and preserve the faith." Devils seduce more women than men, because women are a pushover. Easy prey: easy lay.

Next it is illustrated from scripture that the emotions of women are also defective. Ecclesiasticus is cited again: "There is no wrath above the wrath of a woman." Following Seneca, nothing is "so much to be feared as the lust and hatred of a woman who has been divorced from the marriage bed." Women are jealous and envious: Sarah of Hagar (Genesis 21), Rachel of Leah (Genesis 30), Hannah of Peninnah (1 Kings 1), Miriam of Moses' unnamed Ethiopian wife (Numbers 12), and Martha of Mary (Luke 10:38–42). Another verse, "Neither consult with a woman touching her of whom she is jealous" (Ecclesiasticus 37:11), leads to the conclusion that "there is always jealousy, that is, envy, in a wicked woman."

The calumnies mount up. Defective intelligence makes them gullible to temptation. They have "weak memories" and cannot learn from experience. They have no sense of discipline. Citing Valerius, the authors warn "that a woman is beautiful to look upon, contaminating to the touch, and deadly to keep." Her "gait, posture, and habit" are "vanity of vanities." The authors choose a verse from Ecclesiastes and then heap their prejudices upon it: "And I find more bitter than death the woman, whose heart is snares and nets, and her hands as bands: whoso pleaseth God shall escape from her; but the sinner shall be taken by her" (Ecclesiastes 7:26).

In the *Malleus* the definite article (*the* woman) becomes indefinite (*a* woman) who then stands for all women, and the phrase "more bitter than death" generates a clutch of different meanings. Men are right to feel extreme bitterness against women, because women try harder to please and seduce men than godly men try to please God. Men are right to feel bitter against women, because women brought sin into the world, and with sin came death (the arguments of Romans 5–8 and 1 Timothy 2:8–15 are in mind here). On this basis the authors argue: "And as the sin of Eve would not have brought death to our soul and body unless the sin had afterwards passed on to Adam, to which he was tempted by Eve, not by the devil, therefore she is more bitter than death." The connection between the heart of a woman and a net is next explained: "it speaks of the inscrutable malice which reigns in their hearts." And there are other reasons for this judgment too. Death is a natural event, "but the sin which arose from woman destroys the soul by depriving it of grace." Men are innocent in relation to the arrival of sin in the world. Or again, death is "an open and terrible enemy, but woman is a wheedling and secret enemy." The second enemy is said to be worse than the first so, once more, womankind is more bitter than death.

The imagery of Ecclesiastes 7:26 is now unpacked with particular reference to witches and their crimes. Hands as bands? "When they place their hands on a creature to bewitch it, then with the help of the devil they perform their design." The "snare of hunters"? That is "the snare of devils." It is bad enough for men to be "caught" merely by the sight of a woman or by her voice. Witches "cast wicked spells on countless men and animals," and these are yet harder to resist.

The cumulative case against women now reaches its climax: "To conclude. All witchcraft comes from carnal lust, which is in women insatiable." The clincher is a warped appeal to Proverbs 30:15–16: "There are three things that are never satisfied, yea, four things say not, It is enough: The grave; and the barren womb; the earth that is not filled with water; and the fire that saith not, It is enough." The second of these is transformed. The intense desire for children and the aching disappointment that they do not arrive is transformed to depict the ravenous demand of women for penetrative sex, if not with obliging men, then with eager devils ("Wherefore for the sake of fulfilling their lusts they consort even with devils"). The argument closes with an appeal to the male gender of Jesus, by which men are spared the desire of copulating with demons: "And blessed be the Highest Who has so far preserved the male sex from so great a crime: for since He was willing to be born and to suffer for us, therefore He has granted to men this privilege."

The *Malleus* was a Catholic work, but it should not be thought that disagreement between Catholic and Protestant spread to the identification, persecution, and judicial murder of witches. The record of Protestant countries makes equally distressing reading (and in some Catholic countries it hardly occurred). The behavior of the Kirk in Scotland was especially despicable.[19] James Dalrymple, a dour Presbyterian, explains why, even if someone identified as a witch were completely harmless, she should still be put to death. Why? Because there is an "obediential obligation" to do so. What is that? It is something "put upon men by the will of God." The killing of witches is one such obligation. God has commanded that witches should not be permitted to live. "For the command, 'Thou shalt not suffer a witch to live' takes place, though the witch have committed no malefice against the life or goods of man."[20] There can be no doubt that this command became a savage text, along with all the others piously cited in the *Malleus*.

Learning from the Legacy?

Twenty centuries of Bible reading did nothing to prevent the persecution of Jews in those centuries, culminating in the unspeakable death camps. Luther inherited anti-Semitism; he did not invent it out of the Bible. But there is much in the New Testament that encouraged anti-Semitism in the first place, and the renewed authority of the Bible and to the "plain sense" (see chapter 7) of scripture at the time of the Reformation, naturalized centuries of hatred and gave it explicit legitimation. Evidence that Luther's anti-Semitism was not unique is found in the lamentable Catholic record against the Jews (which to some extent has been frankly acknowledged).[21] Christians have real cause for sorrow that their tradition has expressed itself so cruelly towards Jews. An implication of genuine sorrow should surely be a determination never again to use the Bible in such a way. *Any* use of the Bible in the service of hatred condemns itself. In the face of so dreadful a misuse of the Bible by Protestants and Catholics in relation to the Jews, who can have any faith at all in the combined poor arguments of these sectors of Christendom in relation to homosexual men and women? They suffered grievously in the death camps too.

Writing this book has confirmed the terrible consequences of skewed Bible-reading. The issue is too important to be left to Church leaders and their theologians. The way Christians read the Bible has potentially serious and perhaps devastating consequences, not just for other Christians, but also for the natural and human worlds. Christians have grown accustomed to thinking that there are Islamic readings of the Qur'an which are dangerous for all humanity, without perhaps acknowledging the extent to which their own scriptures have become savage texts.

The *Malleus* does not invent misogyny. It intensifies an element of the Christian tradition that draws on certain Bible passages and uses these to reinforce socio-cultural norms as these affect women, that is, their being continually in the power of men. The *Malleus* oddly and sinisterly suggests itself as an exemplary work which combines scripture, tradition, and reason (the hallowed sources of theology in Anglicanism!) in creative, practical ways. The short fragment just examined contains 35 biblical references, the majority of them full quotations, and all of them "on message" in that they are made to support a scandalous view of half of humanity. Tradition is used in a reverent and scholarly manner. Judicious quotations are woven into the fabric of the text from Jerome, Chrysostom, Augustine, Gregory, and Bernard, all of whose misogynistic credentials are beyond question. The authors give equal weight to reason. They draw extensively on classical authors, and they use scholastic reasoning extensively. It is a well-balanced work, and as we have seen, it pretends to balance in its treatment of its subject.

A conclusion to be drawn from this is nearly as unpalatable as the content of the work itself. The most renowned theologians, the highest Catholic authorities, and the most scrupulous of theological methods guarantee nothing. St. Paul knew this: "though I have all faith, so that I could remove mountains, and have not charity, I am nothing" (1 Corinthians 13:2). This work spits its approved hatred of women into the dangerous world of late medieval Europe to the detriment of many thousands of innocent victims.[22] The Western world has done much in the last century to undo its disrespect for women. But this disrespect lingers on in the churches. Gender remains a major cause of intra-evangelical disagreement. Men argue about the place of women in the different denominations, much as heterosexuals (real or pretended) argue about the place of homosexuals. Wherever women are required to wear hats, or keep quiet, or are forbidden to teach, or read the Gospel, or enter ordained ministry, or preside at the Eucharist, the old misogyny reasserts itself. The weaker sex cannot represent the male Christ. It continues to constitute a dangerous lack. It must be controlled. While different biblical texts may be used, misogyny remains. Worse, "In western and southern Africa, the large-scale killing of witches has emerged in certain societies, and this is a direct borrowing from the western Christian inheritance, with little precedent in indigenous African cultures."[23]

It may be said that the two books charged with savagery in this chapter are extreme and should therefore not be used as examples of typical historical Bible use. Why not? That they *are* extreme does not justify their concealment. Extreme examples often offer the clearest lessons. Hatred of anyone can never be right, and where theology is used to justify it, and God is invoked to vindicate it, there is bad theology and blasphemy. If we could assume that all Christians nowadays wished to renounce anti-Semitism, it would still be necessary to study its origins and its transmission through past Christian belief and practice, not to conceal them, in order to overcome an inheritance that has blighted two millennia and must not blight another one.

Could the two issues of anti-Semitism and sexism have been dealt with differently? Part III argues for a theology which is Christocentric but not bibliocentric, and within the former lies the possibility of very different treatments. Paul's argument that God has incorporated the Gentiles into the people God has chosen through Christ (Romans 9–11), who represents the whole of humanity before God (1 Corinthians 15:22) and who reconciles the whole of humanity with God (2 Corinthians 5:19), is based on sound theology and **Christology**.

If the whole of humanity is reconciled to God, how can the Jewish people no longer be reconciled to God? Again according to Paul, God has conquered the power of sin and death through the death and resurrection of Christ (Romans 5–8). Sexism and its more extreme version, misogyny, belong to the category of *social* or *structural* sin, because they have diminished and invalidated half the human race. Christians joyfully proclaim a new order where sin is overcome, and the apparatuses for its transmission are dismantled. Christian theology, that is, theology which puts the Word before the word, can do things very differently.

There are many other examples of savage Bible use that could have been described. Millions of young men have been driven to unnecessary guilt and despair by the false belief that when they took pleasure in their bodies by masturbating, they were committing the grave sin of onanism, for which God's punishment was death (Genesis 38:7–9). The harsh sentencing of criminals in "the rush to punish,"[24] in the United States and Britain, is almost certainly due to the influence of Old Testament **retributivism** upon the Protestant mind.[25] A whole chapter could, and perhaps should, have been included on the wretched connections made between various human disabilities and the sense that such calamities are God's just punishment for sin (not necessarily one's own).[26] The influence of creationism upon the development of science undermines the achievements of Christians in wishing to contribute, in an academically respectable and necessary way, to the urgent interdisciplinary conversations between theology and science that need to be had. But readers will be familiar with the argument by now. Appeal to the Bible guarantees nothing, and may license all manner of savagery. It is time to inquire further into the excessive veneration of the Bible that produces these disastrous results, and to suggest possibilities for alternative readings.

Part III

Beyond the Text: Faith in the Triune God

Part II produced a catalog of issues where the "plain sense" or the "literal sense" of scripture has contributed to all manner of cruelty, violence, and prejudice. There must be "a more excellent way" (as Paul said when comparing "charity" with the secondary charismatic gifts – 1 Corinthians 12:31) of reading the Bible than those we have so far considered. Part III suggests such a way.

7

Faith in the Book or Faith in God?

The story of the Bible in Protestantism is complicated and contested, and engagement with it here is limited to the attempt, however cursory, to make sense of the extraordinary and counter-Christian results of its interpretation encountered in part II. Protestants, of course, do not have a monopoly of savage interpretation: Catholics are capable of savage interpretation of both scripture *and* tradition (as the *Malleus Maleficarum* has just shown). The first half of this chapter deconstructs the inflation of the Protestant Scripture Principle on which modern biblicism rests. This deconstruction is, however, positive, because it paves the way for a positive endorsement (in chapter 8) of Luther's attempt "to test every Scripture by whether 'it sets forth Christ or not.'"[1] In the second half the account of the Bible provided by the Anglican Richard Hooker (1554–1600) is commended for contemporary use in the Church. Next the common Christian assumption that the boundaries of scripture are fixed, that is, that the canon is closed, is examined and found wanting. Finally, it is suggested that the "lost Christianities" revealed in non-canonical writings reinforce the need to adopt a more open, inclusive, and charitable stance toward alternative versions of the Catholic faith, past and present.

Protestantism is above all a *protest* against idolatry in all its forms. That protest was believed to be authorized by the commandment "Thou shalt not make unto thee any graven image, or any likeness of any thing that is in heaven above, or that is in the earth beneath, or that is in the water under the earth" (Exodus 20:4). (It cannot even be said whether this is the second commandment or a continuation of the first commandment, since the ancient disagreement over this left even the Reformed churches and the Lutheran churches on opposing sides.) The argument of this book leads to the conclusion that bible-centered versions of the Protestant tradition, having smashed or removed the images from the churches of Europe and built new ones, often visually unchallenging and purposefully drab, have created a "graven image" or idol more insidious than any statue or stained-glass window that could not be tolerated by the Reformed conscience. That idol *is* the Bible itself, now elevated to a divine Book through which God "speaks" (almost as if Christ had never come). How ironic that the descendants of the movement which in the name of the Bible crusaded against idolatry have now produced for themselves an Idol which millions of Christians worship.

The Scripture Principle

A founding principle of the Protestant Reformation is the Scripture Principle. This is where the elevation of the Bible to ultimacy begins. The principle resides in the slogan *sola scriptura* ("by scripture alone"). The slogan is, of course, exclusive. The faith and practice of the Church, and of each member of it, are to be determined by scripture alone. So faith and practice are to be determined neither by tradition, nor by reason, nor by the Church. The Reformers agreed that there were many beliefs and practices of the Catholic Church that scripture could not support. These included the sale of **indulgences**, the transubstantiation of bread and wine at the Mass into the body and blood of Christ,[2] the place of "**works**" in acquiring salvation, the legitimacy of five of the seven sacraments of the Church (only baptism and the Eucharist survive), prayers and masses for the dead, praying to the saints, and much else. The papal office could not be justified either, *sola scriptura* (despite the customary understanding of the saying of Jesus to the apostle Peter: "thou art Peter, and upon this rock I will

114

build my church; and the gates of hell shall not prevail against it" [Matthew 16:18]). What the Church teaches is open to constant correction by, or in the light of, scripture. The authority of the Church is thus subject to the authority of scripture, and scripture alone.

Which Scriptures?

"Here I stand; I can do no other," is "the most memorable thing Luther *never* said."[3] Nonetheless, writes MacCulloch, it "can stand for the motto of all Protestants – ultimately, perhaps, of all western civilization."[4] Since Luther (1483–1546) takes his stand on scripture alone, what scripture or scriptures was he talking about? Which translation? What *is* scripture? How can the Church, to which the scriptures belong, get scripture wrong, and if it does, how are they to be interpreted aright? For more than a thousand years the Church relied on the Vulgate, an early fifth-century Latin translation of Hebrew and Greek editions of the biblical books undertaken largely by Jerome (around 340–420 CE). But in 1516 **Erasmus** produced a Greek version of the New Testament which showed that Jerome's Latin translation had made several unjustifiable assumptions, on some of which hitherto unchallengeable Catholic doctrine rested.[5] In the 1380s John Wyclif had translated the Vulgate into English. In 1526 the first ever edition of the New Testament in the English language was published, translated by William Tyndale (1494–1536). While the Bible was becoming available in the vernacular (as the Vulgate itself once was!) the Catholic Church feared the consequences of untutored reading and unauthorized interpretation. That is why the Council of Trent (1546) "ordains and declares, that the said old and vulgate edition, which, by the lengthened usage of so many years, has been approved of in the Church, be, in public lectures, disputations, sermons and expositions, held as authentic; and that no one is to dare, or presume to reject it under any pretext whatever."[6]

The cry *sola scriptura* is therefore muted by the difficulty of specifying which *version* of the scriptures was to be used. Equally problematic was the canonical question, "Which scriptures?" There is little recognition

115

today of the uncertainty that this question engendered. For a thousand years the books Protestants know only (if at all) as **Apocrypha** and which are excluded from their Bibles, had been regarded as fully canonical. At a stroke they were removed. The Anglican churches list them outside the canon but retain them "for example of life and instruction of manners."[7] Here is a disagreement no nearer to resolution than it was nearly 500 years ago. More seriously, are *all* the books, even in the New Testament, indisputably canonical? Modern biblicists may find it difficult to discover that Luther did not include Hebrews, the Letters of James and Jude, and Revelation among the "right, sure principal books," and he separated them out from the other 23 books in his September Bible of 1522. Erasmus doubted the authenticity of 2 and 3 John as well; Zwingli thought Revelation should be rejected, and Calvin had doubts about 2 Peter and Revelation.[8] So much for agreement about which books comprise our Bible.

All Scriptures Equal?

If doctrine and practice are to be determined *sola scriptura*, is each scripture equally valuable, and to be regarded as equal in authority with others in the canon? Clearly the Reformers thought not. Luther thought the Letter of James contradicted Paul's doctrine of **justification by faith**, on which the Reformation arguably depended. But many evangelicals and all Christian fundamentalists will have no truck with the need for selectivity among the scriptures (even though they are highly selective themselves). In this as in much else they *agree* with Rome, for the Council of Trent declared it "receives and venerates *with an equal affection of piety, and reverence*, all the books both of the Old and of the New Testament,"[9] including those relegated to the Protestant Apocrypha. A more honest and pragmatic view of the selective use of scripture is provided by Karl Barth, who admits that "the Church as a whole, as it has made its mind known in its symbols, confessional writings, its theology, preaching and devotional literature, does not in fact and practice treat all parts of the Bible alike, or without tacit questions in relation to one or other of them."[10] That is certainly not the view of the fundamentalists, for whom the Word of God is verbally and uniformly inspired. Neither was it the view of the Council of Trent, for "if any one receive not, as sacred and canonical, the said books *entire with all their parts*, as they have been used to be read in the Catholic Church, and as they are contained in the old Latin vulgate edition; and knowingly and deliberately contemn the traditions aforesaid; let him be **anathema**."

Scripture Interprets Scripture?

If the Catholic Church was in error, how could any Christian or group of Christians validly decide that it was? This question is traditionally discussed among Protestants as a question of rivalry or priority between "the Bible" and "the Church." On a historical/chronological view there is no case to answer. There were Christians, and so a Church, before there were any written Christian records, and the canon, when it was finally agreed (before being reopened at the Reformation) is clearly a decision of the Church. But if the Bible is to judge the Church (the *sola scriptura* principle requires this), how is it done? Must there not be some accredited authority, some agency of interpretation, that gets the Bible right and shows the Church to be wrong? Yet how could there be?

The lame answer, of course, is that scripture is its own interpreter. How can it do that? That would be an impossible feat. It thinly conceals that *people* interpret the Bible. There is no way the Bible can interpret itself without dissenting interpreters, and interpreters have notoriously dissented not only from the historic Church, but from each other's rival dissenting views. The Protestant scripture principle has to allow another, the principle of *private judgment*, according to which (and despite disclaimers from the guardians of Protestant orthodoxy) anyone can figure out the meaning of scripture for themselves. Of course, they should seek the guidance of the Spirit, or look for Christ in the scripture, or pray about its meaning, and so on. But these necessary caveats have not stopped bizarre private judgments, egocentric and callous interpretations, and the parading of intolerance

117

and ignorance in the guise of inspiration. Again the Council of Trent yields nothing to the principle of private judgment:

> Furthermore, in order to restrain petulant spirits, It decrees, that no one, relying on his own skill, shall – in matters of faith, and of morals pertaining to the edification of Christian doctrine – wresting the sacred Scripture to his own senses, presume to interpret the said sacred Scripture contrary to that sense which holy mother Church – whose it is [*sic*] to judge of the true sense and interpretation of the holy Scriptures – hath held and doth hold.

The "Literal Sense"?

Another consequence of the *sola scriptura* principle is the necessity of a literal interpretation of the Bible. If everything is to be decided on the basis of what it appears to say, it must say it, say it plainly, and say it to the hundreds of thousands of new individual readers who are reading the Bible, for the first time and for themselves, in their own language, and equipped with a new status, that of independent readers who, in theory, could be privately illumined just by confronting a biblical text. Despite the obvious fact that many of the words, ideas, and literary forms are metaphorical or symbolic, and often intentionally ambiguous in their very suggestiveness, the Bible is to be understood, wherever possible, literally. Now a new trend emerges: a literal understanding of scripture becomes imposed on alternative readings of scripture, even if what is read is resistant to such insensitive handling. The trend culminates in the rigor of the fundamentalists and the sectarians such as the Jehovah's Witnesses in our own time. Stemming from the literalization of Bible reading are profound consequences which extend beyond all the churches and influence the rise of modern science.

Prior to the Reformation the Church had used a fourfold method for reading the Bible, called the *Quadriga*.[11] There were believed to be four senses which a passage of scripture might be thought to convey,

118

and depending on the passage one or more could be dominant over the others. The first was the *literal* sense. The second was *allegorical*: this sense treated the passage as a sign or extended metaphor whose meaning lay outside the passage itself. (The most obvious example of biblical allegory is the interpretation of the lovers' passion in the Song of Songs as pointing to the love of Christ for the Church.) The third sense was *moral*, conveying something that had to be done, and the fourth was **anagogical**, conveying something to be hoped for. A consequence of the Reformation was the elevation of the literal sense above all the others. But this was no mere shift in devotional preference – it represented a momentous change in the culture of Protestant societies and their universities, for, as Peter Harrison argues, the demise of allegory brought about "a new conception of the world, itself premised on a particular view of the meaning of texts," which "was to drive a wedge between words and things, restricting the allocation of meanings to the former."[12]

Luther's suspicion of allegory was well founded. Allegory allowed biblical interpreters to evade the moral and religious imperatives which required the literal sense. He could scarcely have imagined the consequences of the new literalism on both science and theology. The development of the natural sciences in this period was aided and directly influenced by it. The new emerging scientific world-view, thinks Harrison, "was made possible … by the collapse of the allegorical interpretation of texts." He explains why. The denial of the legitimacy of allegory was "in essence a denial of the capacity of things to act as signs. The demise of allegory, in turn, was due largely to the efforts of Protestant reformers, who in their search for an unambiguous religious authority, insisted that the book of scripture be interpreted only its literal, historical sense." It is not the case that the scientists disbelieved what they read in the Bible; rather, "when in the sixteenth century people began to read the Bible in a different way, they found themselves forced to jettison traditional conceptions of the world."[13] While many factors were responsible for the rise of modern science, "by far the most significant was the literalist mentality initiated by the Protestant reformers, and sponsored by their

119

successors."[14] In 1605 Francis Bacon was to reintroduce the older Two Books theory, the Book of Nature and the Book of Scripture, both of them written by God.[15] Their separation, he argued, would secure the autonomy of science ("natural philosophy") and thus free it from interference from the Church and theology. But the metaphor of nature as a book requires it to be understood as a text, with an inquiring reader and a means of understanding what is read. Both books required the literal sense to be uppermost in their readers' minds, and the literal sense of the Book of Nature allowed no transcendental or religious meanings of natural objects into its own canon. Both books of divine knowledge were required to be interrogated by the same scientific principles.[16]

Locked in the Past?

Both the Reformed emphasis on *sola scriptura* and the unreformed Catholic emphasis on the Vulgate version of the Bible in the sixteenth century should be located within a broader attitude to the past that was to serve neither part of the Church well. Such was the hold of classical authorship on the contemporary scientific mind that it could not contemplate innovation without some legitimizing reference to the classical authors, especially Aristotle. Could the ancient authors be wrong, their observations incomplete? "As the sixteenth century progressed, the new knowledge of nature gave rise to challenges to the completeness and accuracy of the ancients. Aristotle's circumscribed world could yield up but a small fraction of what the enlarged globe had now to offer."[17] An unpleasant but revealing example of an excessive veneration of the past is the attitude to the spread of syphilis within Europe at about the same time as Luther's break from Rome. The "French Pocks" as it was known (except in France, where it was known as "the English disease") baffled doctors, yet "Renaissance scholars … seriously debated whether the French pox could exist at all, since it apparently lacked a proper Latin or Greek name … For humanists besotted with classical wisdom it took a leap of the imagination, beyond even most clever people at the time, to suppose that reality could extend beyond the knowledge of a dead philosopher."[18] The explosion of modern knowledge was bound to expose the over-reliance upon the classical authors and their views of the world and what was in it. Christian theology was also caught in this absorbing development. It still is largely preoccupied with the past, its texts and their languages, locked into its fascination with an age long gone. On the one hand the study of the past is vitally necessary to any historical religion like Christianity. On the other, the preoccupation with the past is likely to be evasive, a means of avoiding engagement with the natural and social sciences and with the physical, social, and political (and environmental) worlds of today.

Bible Worship?

In 1611 the Authorized, or King James, version of the Bible became available. It was actually authorized by no one,[19] and about 90 percent of it was a verbatim copy of the highly *un*authorized translation into English of William Tyndale, the early Reformer who was strangled and burned at the stake. Christians brought up with the Bible freely available for them to read in their own language may find it difficult to appreciate the horror with which the unreformed Church regarded being bypassed as the divinely authorized interpreter of scripture. The English philosopher Thomas Hobbes (1588–1679), during whose lifetime the Authorized Version appeared, complained that "Every man, nay, every boy and wench, that could read English thought they spoke with God Almighty, and understood what he said, when by a certain number of chapters a day they had read the Scriptures once or twice over."[20] According to Stephen Katz, the **Puritans** of sixteenth- and seventeenth-century Britain "were convinced that the Bible provided an infallible guide in a wide variety of areas … The end result was to create a climate of *Bible worship* unknown before the emergence of Fundamentalism nearly three hundred years later."[21]

The charge of Bible worship, like that of racism or homophobia, is likely to be resisted, so if it is used of biblicist Christians today it

121

should be cautiously and charitably made. I *do*, however, think that that charge can be upheld. Only *God*, in the Judeo-Christian tradition, is worthy of worship. If the biblical writings are protected from error (assuming we could ever know that), then they *are* divine. To be divine is presumably to be free from error: certainly to be human is to err. That the Bible *is* divine is an assertion I hear many Christians still making, even though the Bible does not claim such lofty status for itself, and the Creeds of the Church know of no such inflated idea. The contrast between the Creator and the creature is fatally compromised if any inspiration the authors may have had protected them from errors. Is it unreasonable to discern bibliolatry among Christians whenever, say, the words of scripture are assigned the same status as that given to the Jesus of the Gospels or the Creeds; whenever the teaching of Moses or Paul is given equal weight (or greater weight in the case of Paul) to the teaching of Jesus; whenever (as the famous Protestant theologian Paul Tillich said of his own tradition) the proximate is raised to ultimacy; when what is not God is confused with what is; or whenever other sources of theology (tradition, reason, experience[22]) are bypassed?

Given the new prominence, in the sixteenth century, of the Old Testament alongside the New, an issue plaguing the Protestant churches was what to do with it! If it was sacred scripture in the same sense as the New Testament, how was the New Testament "new"? A particular example of this was the Ten Commandments (Exodus 20:1–17; Deuteronomy 5:6–21). It was not just that these came to replace the **Seven Deadly Sins** as the benchmark of human wickedness. The commandment forbidding the making of "any graven image" justified the smashing of millions of icons, statues, and windows in the churches of Europe. The commandment to keep the Sabbath day holy (Exodus 20:8), now understood as applying directly and authoritatively to Christian practice, reversed the previous encouragement of recreation and sport on Sunday. However, the conversion of the traditional Sunday into the more austere Sabbath did not settle a different question: on what day should the Sabbath be observed – on the first or the last day of the week?

More Disputed Questions

But *that* question was only one of many that could not be settled *sola scriptura*. We have already seen how the Bible does not settle the deep ethical questions surrounding homosexuality, slavery, and the other issues discussed in part II. Neither could it settle competing claims between Saturday or Sunday being the day of rest. The Bible nowhere mentions Sunday yet there are many references to the Sabbath which, as everyone knew, had always been observed on Saturdays. Was Sunday yet another unscriptural institution the Papists had dreamed up? Certainly the Seventh Day Adventists and Seventh Day Baptists thought, and still think, so. And why not, if the matter is to be settled by scripture alone?

And why, if the Church is to practice only what scripture authorizes, does it continue to baptize children? There is no trace of this practice in the Bible; indeed, the denial of the freedom of the believer to choose baptism for him- or herself may itself be morally dubious. **Baptists** and other Christians of the **radical Reformation** understand this well and witness to it faithfully. Here is a remarkable inconsistency. The Reformed churches were prepared to stake everything on the authority of the Bible, yet they timorously refused to rock the boat over the mode of baptism (immersion) and the constituency (*adults* professing their faith). Luther was not prepared to give an inch on this, even though it was a rare issue on which the Bible was actually clear. The Reformers were driven to the implausibility of finding scriptural authorization for it in the ancient Jewish practice of circumcising young boys! "Just as circumcision had been done under the law as the symbol of entry to the old Israel, so baptism was done under grace for entry to the new Israel."[23] Lutherans and Catholics even co-operated with each other in seeking to extirpate the **Anabaptists** who sought to emulate biblical baptismal practice. An early Anabaptist leader, Balthasar Hubmaier, was burned at the stake for his errors. " 'Salt me, salt me well!' was his brave essay at donnish humour to the executioners as they rubbed gunpowder into his beard and hair." His opponents were not only vicious, they were ironic.

123

The method of execution of his loyal Anabaptist wife added further cruel irony to its cruelty: a stone was placed around her neck and she was drowned in the Danube.[24]

The list could be endlessly extended. While scripture is essential to everything any Christian Church might now or in the future teach, nothing at all can be settled by reference to scripture *alone*. Here is further confirmation of the conclusion of part II. It didn't settle the problem of baptism. Protestants have quietly forgotten that all the Reformers believed in the perpetual virginity of Mary (justified on the basis of flimsy and fanciful proof-texts),[25] in the face of Gospel references to the brothers and sisters of Jesus. Would it not be as likely a possibility to find a recipe for apple pie in the Bible as to find a statement of support for Mary's continuing virginity? It would not be long before the proof-text for the virgin birth of Jesus (Matthew 1:23) would be assailed for being a mistranslation of the Hebrew which it quoted. The Scottish Calvinists even wanted for a time to keep the shops *open* on Christmas Day on the grounds that feast days were not biblically authorized.[26] That the Bible doesn't deliver on any of these matters should be sufficient reason to abandon the misguided expectation that it does, or ever can. Of course, once "tradition" is added to the Christian sources of revelation on which the churches may draw (chapter 8), some plausibility is restored to the earlier beliefs, including some of those that the Reformers overthrew. The *sola scriptura* doctrine provides no plausibility at all, yet this is the strand of Reformed teaching that retains its greatest influence over the modern-day biblicists.

Hooker and the Middle Way

Anglicans and Episcopalians today who are struggling with biblicism throughout the Anglican Communion can learn much from the arguments against the Calvinists and the Puritans put forward by one of the "founders" of Anglican theology, Richard Hooker. He insists on the authority of the Church over the interpretation of the Bible. Taking his stand on Anglican teaching that "Holy Scripture containeth all things necessary to salvation,"[27] he observes that without the Church we would not know what scripture was; neither could scripture tell us. We first need to know "how the books of Holy Scripture contain in them all necessary things, when of things necessary the very chiefest is to know what books we are bound to esteem holy; which point is confessed impossible for the Scripture itself to teach."[28] Scripture is, and remains, the Church's book. Next, in order to know what things are necessary we also need to know what things are *not* necessary. There is a great deal of stage-setting required (as Wittgenstein might have said) before we can tell the difference, and the Church provides this. Next he asks what it means to say that Scripture "contains" these necessary things. The doctrine of the Trinity and the practice of infant baptism are necessary, he avers, but scripture does not directly teach either. "For our belief in the Trinity ... the duty of baptizing infants: these with such other principal points, the necessity whereof is by none denied, are notwithstanding in Scripture no where to be found by express literal mention, only deduced they are out of Scripture by collection."[29]

Hooker would have approved of the emphasis in this volume on the purpose of scripture to be a witness to Jesus Christ. He adopts for the Bible the explicit purpose that St. John adopted for his Gospel: "These things are written, that ye might believe that Jesus is Christ the Son of God, and that in believing ye might have life through his name" (John 20:31). "The main drift of the whole New Testament," he says, "is that which St. John setteth down as the purpose of his own history," while "The drift of the Old [is] that which the Apostle mentioneth to Timothy, 'The Holy Scriptures are able to make thee wise unto Salvation'" (2 Timothy 3:15). Both Testaments are alike in bearing witness to Christ, and different in how they do it – "So that the general end both of Old and New is one; the difference between them consisting in this, that the Old did make wise by teaching salvation through Christ that should come, the New by teaching that Christ the Saviour *is* come."[30]

Hooker also sounds contemporary when he treats of the relation of scripture to other matters, three of which must command our attention.

In a series of poems in Proverbs 1–9, Wisdom is personified as a woman. Indeed in these chapters she is a mediator between God and humanity and God's companion before the world was created (Proverbs 3:19, 8:22–31). Hooker affirms and continues the personification of wisdom when he places "Her" above the Two Books, those of Nature and Scripture. He says:

> As her ways are of sundry kinds, so her manner of teaching is not merely one and the same. Some things she openeth by the sacred books of Scripture; some things by the glorious works of Nature: with some things she inspireth them from above by spiritual influence; in some things she leadeth and traineth them only by world experience and practice. We may not so in any one special kind admire her, that we disgrace her in any other; but let all her ways be according unto their place and degree adored.[31]

On the one hand Hooker is continuing, almost playfully, the poetic license he finds in Proverbs. On the other hand, Wisdom is the divine teacher who sits above scripture and nature and uses both to illumine us as she chooses. Like God the Spirit she can inspire us to know the things that Nature does not disclose to us. She teaches us through scripture, yet she also teaches us as we engage in the commercial, political, and social domains ("world experience and practice") and learn from her there. If we look to scripture only to receive instruction from divine Wisdom, we wrongly admire her in "one special kind."

Second, when challenged by the Calvinists to find biblical grounds for everything a Christian does, Hooker responded that there are some things which are "neither to be commanded nor forbidden, but left free and arbitrary."[32] These are matters that are "indifferent," that is, because they are non-essential to the faith, difference with regard to them is expected and permitted. This principle of indifference or *adiaphora* is essential for a loving, tolerant church that welcomes diversity among its members, and it is a great disappointment that the churches which comprise the Anglican Communion did not adopt it with regard to their differences over homosexuality which "impaired" communion between them.[33] Third, Hooker ridicules the assumption that an appeal to scripture can by itself settle what Catholic teaching is and what heresy is. If that were true, Hooker asks, in relation to the many classical disputes in Church history, "what madness was it with such kinds of proofs to nourish their contention, when there were such effectual means to end all controversy that was between them!"[34]

What Happened to the Originals?

Hooker (and other early Anglican theologians) provides a basis for exposing the bibliolatry of his opponents. The position he criticized in 1593 is very much less plausible now than it was then, even though millions of Christians continue to be captivated by it. The arrival of the Authorized Version and its huge influence contributed greatly to the establishment of the myth of the stable text of scripture in English-speaking countries. (That was a reason for using it in this volume.) Yet the steady increase in the number of biblical manuscripts led to a steady increase in the knowledge of comparative differences between them. When John Mill produced his Greek New Testament in 1707, after 30 years of intense work based on the manuscript evidence then available to him, his work had "a cataclysmic effect," not least because it "isolated some thirty *thousand* places of variation among the surviving manuscripts."[35] There was dismay at the publication of this version precisely because it would weaken further the *sola scriptura* dogma. In 2003 Bart Ehrman estimated the number of differences between extant manuscripts to be somewhere between 200,000 and 300,000! The figure is vague because no one has been able to count them. He says "Perhaps it is simplest to express the figure in comparative terms: There are more differences among our manuscripts than there are words in the New Testament."[36]

Biblical manuscripts unknown to the Reformers provide a mass of new information about the diversity of, and the controversies within, the Christianity of the first few hundred years. They are not such good news for people who think the originals were directly "inspired" in some way. At the very least the wealth of manuscript material draws attention to our lack of originals, for "What we have are copies

127

of the originals or, to be more accurate, copies made from copies of the copies of the copies of the originals. Most of these surviving copies are hundreds of years removed from the originals themselves."[37] Bible translators now have hundreds more manuscripts, hundreds of years older than those available to the producers of the Authorized Version. It is open to the biblicists to argue that God nevertheless inspired the originals – since their hypothesis does not rest on evidence, it remains intact. But then, since the whole matter is nothing to do with evidence and must be approached *a priori*, so to speak, what is that hypothesis worth? It is, of course, a matter of faith, and that is why it comes close to bibliolatry. The Gospel summons is to people to have faith in what God has done for the world through Christ. It is not faith in a book, not even in a very holy book, to which we are summoned, but to faith in *God*. If God had intended God's faithful followers to witness to an originally inspired Bible, could not and would not God preserve what God had, albeit by human hand, written down?

A further question that is difficult for the biblicists to answer is why the changes came about. While some of them are the innocent mistakes of copyists (there are lots of those), others are changes deliberately introduced by partisan Christians later on in order to influence the outcome of controversies and settle them in their favor. These changes are well enough known to students of the New Testament, and some of them are summarized simply by Ehrman.[38] The earliest accounts of the baptism of Jesus favor the belief that God "adopted" Jesus as the "Beloved Son" at the baptism itself. The accounts are changed to favor the later orthodox view that Jesus was Son of God from conception. Some **Gnostic** Christians separated out the divine and human elements in the one Christ. Some of the texts they used in order to do this were subtly altered. Other changes may have been made to counter an opposite tendency, that of the **Docetists**, who denied that Jesus was human at all. These later alterations greatly assist the reconstruction of Christian belief and its development, but they assist the "inspirationists" not one whit. Which versions are inspired? Presumably the earliest ones. So why were they altered? Were the alterations inspired too?

A Closed Canon?

More perplexing even than the comparative differences between manuscripts is the discovery of lost ones. The early Church argued over the inclusion of Hebrews, 2 Peter, Jude, and Revelation. It also argued over the "runners up." The Letter of 1 Clement, the *Didache*, the Letter of Barnabas, and the Shepherd of Hermas were among these. We have seen how Christians disagreed at the Reformation over what should be included in the canon or list of sacred scripture. But what are we to make of the Gospel of Thomas, discovered in the **Nag Hammadi** library in 1945, and containing 114 sayings of Jesus? A majority of scholars believe its author has preserved some of the actual sayings of Jesus as they were transmitted orally.[39] This book has already been included in at least one current translation of the Christian scriptures.[40] Or the *Didache*, forgotten until rediscovered in 1873 in Constantinople, yet of enormous value in informing us about the doctrine and liturgical practice of (part of) the Church around 100 CE?

An option, by far the most convenient, for the contemporary Church is to affirm that the New Testament is what Athanasius in 367 CE said it was – the 27 books in our modern bibles. These and no others the Holy Spirit inspired. These and no others the Holy Spirit wisely led the Church to accept as canonical. Since the canon is closed, why reopen it? But that position, attractive though it is, ignores too much. First, it ignores the early arguments about the canon (which Athanasius did not settle). Even in Athanasius' home church, Didymus the Blind thought 2 Peter was a forgery and regarded the Shepherd of Hermas and the Letter of Barnabas as "scriptural authorities."[41] The arguments were vigorous, sometimes rancorous. Of course the Holy Spirit can guide as a result of, or in spite of, rancor among Christians and churches. But how do we know that this closure of the canon is due to the Holy Spirit, and not a *post hoc* attempt at a resolution of an intractable difficulty by appeal to divine action or divine authority? (The Holy Spirit declined to preserve some of the writings the Holy Spirit presumably inspired, for example the lost 3 Corinthians, written by Paul.)

129

Second, it ignores the dodgy application of one of the main criteria that was used to determine admission into the canon, namely **apostolicity**. It was entirely appropriate to insist that the canonical books should have been written by eyewitnesses to Jesus who heard his teaching for themselves. But who could have believed *the scale of pseudonymity* that this worthy criterion generated? The extent of the forgeries that were permitted, encouraged, accepted? We do not know that the four biblical Gospels were written by Matthew, Mark, Luke, and John. They do not say they were. Apostolic authorship was assigned to them later (Mark being the secretary of one, and Luke the traveling companion of another). A clear majority of scholars think that Paul wrote about half of the 13 letters attributed to him. Revelation survived partly because of its association, through the common **homonym** John (Revelation 1:1), with the author of the fourth Gospel. There are disputes about the authorship of Hebrews, James, and 2 Peter, and the attribution of 1 Peter and Jude to, respectively, the apostle Peter and to the brother of Jesus are also strongly contested. The early Christians did not intend to deceive, but they did not share our modern criteria of authenticity. The modern Church, however, needs to accommodate the discovery that the *human* authorship of most of the New Testament books is shrouded in uncertainty. Is it not harder to assign divine inspiration to the human authors of these texts if we do not know who these authors were?

Third, that the Holy Spirit inspired these unknown authors is a possibility that appears to overlook the variation in quality within the writings themselves. Of course the suggestion invites the retort that God can inspire the authors to say what God wants them to say, and that we ought to obey the Bible and be judged by it, rather than judge it (and find it wanting). Luther (unwisely in my view) found James "a right strawy epistle," but what can be said of Jude? Well, one commentator finds it "rich in content, owing to its masterly composition and its economy of expression,"[42] yet the book is devoted to the condemnation and damnation of fellow Christians for their alleged sexual misadventures. (Incidentally, Jude quotes authoritatively from a book found in neither the Roman Catholic nor the Protestant canon – 1 Enoch.) But sexual slander was almost an art form (or at any rate a "rhetorical strategy"[43]) in the ancient world (as Jennifer Knust has shown). Power struggles commonly proceeded by assigning weakness of character to opponents, and a common way of throwing mud at them and making it stick was to sign up to self-mastery and accuse opponents of debauchery. "Once the legitimacy of a position or a group has been linked to a particular definition of sexual virtue, accusations of sexual vice become a potent weapon for distinguishing insiders from outsiders, policing group boundaries, and eliminating rivals."[44] Jude sets a frankly deplorable moral standard of argument for rival Christian groups to attend to their disagreements, and assumes an exclusivity of doctrine and practice which tolerates no rivals. It sets the tone for the bickering that still goes on as ecclesiastical boundaries are policed today. There are better ways of loving one's neighbor, especially when they are brothers and sisters in Christ, than consigning them to "the blackness of darkness for ever" (Jude 13). It is important that Christians should not assign to the Holy Spirit the warrant for treating their brothers and sisters in the family of God with the arrogance, hatred, and dismissal that assert themselves in this pseudonymous work.

Fourth, a closed canon heightens the contrast between what the Spirit inspires and does not inspire. Did the inspiration of the Holy Spirit cease when the 27 books were completed? Here the Roman Catholic Church is on stronger ground in affirming "a close connection and communication between sacred tradition and Sacred Scripture. For both of them, flowing from the same divine wellspring, in a certain way merge into a unity and tend toward the same end." "Sacred tradition and Sacred Scripture form one sacred deposit of the word of God."[45] (Yet few Protestants, Anglo-Catholics included, will follow Catholic orthodoxy into the further claim that "the task of authentically interpreting the word of God, whether written or handed on, has been entrusted exclusively to the living teaching office of the Church, whose authority is exercised in the name of Jesus Christ.")

Finally, there are good reasons for thinking that the formation of the canon did not take place as it has been traditionally understood. The standard version is that the Catholic faith, "once delivered unto the saints" (Jude 3), has been preserved from error by the zealous advocacy of Catholic Christians who have protected it from countless heretics. These heretics have "crept in unawares" (Jude 4) and sought to distort it, motivated variously by lust, the Devil, ambition, spiritual blindness, and so on. The problem with this account is that, like most official historical accounts, it is written by the victorious party which then proclaims its own truth against the errors of its opponents. That, however, is not the whole story. The crude claim that "truth is power" overlooks the point that good arguments also have a power of their own, and I think that a good, intellectual, coherent, and humble case can be made for saying that Catholic doctrine as it came to be expressed in the classical Creeds of the Church makes the best sense of the Word of God given in Christ and continually reinterpreted in the Church through the Spirit. But there can be little doubt that the triumph of orthodoxy took place at the expense of other Christian groups and traditions which were often misrepresented and sometimes persecuted or extirpated. It is possible and necessary both to be thankful for the preservation and development of the faith, and at the same time to extend the love God shows us in Christ to doctrinal opponents, then and now. What hope can there be for charitable conversations between the religions if there cannot be charitable conversations between Christians, their churches, and their skeptical neighbors?

"Lost Christianities" and New "Heresies"

In learning again how to treat Christians of a different persuasion with due solicitude, the "lost Christianities" that Ehrman describes have much to teach us. There is, he concludes,

> a sense that alternative understandings of Christianity from the past can be cherished yet today, that they can provide insights even now for those of us who are concerned about the world and our place in it. Those captivated with this fascination commonly feel a sense of loss

upon realizing just how many perspectives once endorsed by well-meaning, intelligent, and sincere believers came to be abandoned, destroyed, and forgotten – as were the texts that these believers produced, read, and revered.[46]

Well: these non-canonical texts included 17 Gospels, five Acts of the Apostles, 13 letters and related writings, and seven Apocalypses.[47] And the sincere believers included the **Marcionites**, the **Ebionites**, the **Montanists**, and the **Arians**. In fact these unorthodox Christians have their modern counterparts in the contemporary Church, and a more sympathetic re-evaluation of them might rekindle sympathy for them in our time. Who cannot but feel sympathy for Marcion as he found himself revolted by parts of the Old Testament, such as the ones that were considered in part II? What morally sensitive Christian has not at times wondered whether this god was not the Father of Jesus but some other, ancient, warrior god? Indeed it might be a mark of spiritual maturity to disavow all links to this god! The point is: it is possible to have sympathy with and respect for non-Catholic Christians and still believe they were, or are, wrong. Marcion did not have the theory of progressive revelation to help him contextualize his disgust. Marcion was wrong because the New Testament makes no sense without the Old: because its sense of the one God, of the world as a creation, of the voices of the prophets who interpreted the great themes of righteousness and justice in terms of Israel's poor and neglected people is unique and a priceless contribution to the Christian inheritance; and for countless other reasons. Yet people who are discomforted by parts of the Old Testament today are not heretics. Their discomfort may already be a sign of their inkling that the Love revealed by Jesus represents a "fullness" that has no antecedent.

The Ebionites also have their modern counterparts. They may have descended from the opponents of St. Paul against whom the apostle rails in his letters. At the other end of the spectrum from the Marcionites they wanted to retain all things Jewish, including male circumcision. Well, why not? Christians appeal to Old Testament law when deciding who can marry whom (the Prohibited Degrees of marriage); biblicists unhesitatingly appeal to Levitical texts when condemning homosexual sex. The Puritans resemble the Ebionites in their elevation of the Hebrew scriptures to Word of God status. Although they never advocated circumcision, they advocated a "type" of circumcision in the hopeless biblical case for infant baptism. The answer, of course, is loud and clear in Paul's writings: Christ is the fulfillment of the law, and so the law is no longer binding on Christians, but it takes a particular and retrospective position to think that Paul was right. Substantial numbers of Christians thought he was wrong: were they any less true followers of Christ?

The Montanists resemble the modern-day **Pentecostalists** and some of the millennialists of our times. Their emphasis on the immediate fulfillment of prophecy; their revivalist style of preaching, strict personal morality, and the experience of the Holy Spirit in ecstasy all have their parallels in branches of modern fundamentalism. The early Adoptionists may be more faithful to the synoptic Gospels than the orthodox whose Christology eventually won the day. They believed that God "adopted" Jesus as the Son at his baptism. This came to be seen as an inadequate view, yet the writers of the synoptic Gospels may have held that view themselves. Arians mounted a strong, biblically based case for the view that the divinity of Jesus was inconsistent with the monotheistic belief in one God. I remain convinced that the belief that Jesus is truly divine and truly human (*vere deus vere homo*) changes the human understanding of who and what God is, decisively and for ever (and once wrote a book celebrating the "thinkability" of this alleged impossibility[48]). Yet there are many Christians past and present who believe that God acted decisively in Jesus, without Jesus himself being identical with God (as the Catholic faith wisely teaches). These Christians are not confined to the ranks of **Unitarians** and Quakers (whose work for the Kingdom of God is acknowledged inside and outside the churches), but are included among the millions who struggle with the supernatural framework within which classical Christianity continues to express itself. One contemporary theologian (John Hick) who has done more than most to promote inter-religious understanding is clearly a modern-day Arian in his doctrine of God. I disagree with him, yet his voluminous writings on inter-faith dialog embody a profound willingness to recognize the Spirit of God within and among the non-Christian faith traditions, and also to recognize that the **exclusivism** of Christianity has too often offended by its dogmatism and its spiritual blindness in failing to find Christ in "the Other." These are the fruits of a deep Christian understanding, heretical or not.

Avoiding Violence

Standard versions of the eventual settlement of doctrinal disagreements and of the closure of the canon are likely to miss out much of the power politics in which they were immersed. A similar omission is likely in standard versions of the Reformation. If those events are recorded from the point of view of Church history, or of the history of doctrine, it becomes possible to describe them with little or no reference to the appalling and sustained violence in which they were entwined and which they partly caused. It must be charitably assumed that Protestants and Catholics have little idea of the carnage that was inflicted on European people in the sixteenth and seventeenth centuries. Protestants murdered Catholics. Catholics murdered Protestants. Luther, at the time of the Peasants' Revolt, advocated their "private and public murder."[49] Catholics and Protestants united in the horrible persecution of Anabaptists. Calvin approved of the burning of his opponent, Michael Servetus.[50] Lutherans and Calvinists frequently expressed hatred towards each other.[51] Calvinists persecuted Calvinists. Christians persecuted Jews. The Catholic struggle against the Protestants in 1618 "brought thirty years of misery to millions of Europeans," during which 20 to 40 percent of the population of Europe "met an early death through the fighting or the accompanying famine or disease."[52] Even before 1500 "western Christianity must rank as one of the most intolerant religions in world history: its record in comparison with medieval Islamic civilization is embarrassingly poor."[53] After the Reformation it is no surprise that the citizens of Europe gradually dissociated themselves from it.

The relation between religion and war is complex, and the popular identification of one as the cause of the other is simplistic and inadequate, not least because it fails to recognize the link between religion and the role of national and ethnic identity.[54] Our interest lies with the question whether biblicism opens up a new line of justification for violence. On the one hand, the answer is No. Catholics are not biblicists, yet they were responsible for the murder of thousands of Protestants. On the other hand, during and after the Reformation, the direct appeal to the Bible undoubtedly led to all kinds of conclusions, many of them, as we have seen, violent. It is hard to find the signature of the Holy Spirit in either the zeal of Reformers or the intransigence of the Catholics.

The Scripture Principle has been found inadequate in this chapter for several reasons. Additionally, it contributed to the violence that was the Reformation, and its use ever since has enabled some Christians to bypass other sources of theology, and to dumb down their responsive and responsible living of the Love Commandments of Jesus by appealing to scriptures that advocate something different. The New Testament is vital to the faith of Christians, but it is not the foundation of that faith. That foundation is Christ. That is of course sound biblical teaching, explicitly stated by Paul and John. "For other foundation can no man lay than that is laid, which is Jesus Christ" (1 Corinthians 3:11). "Search the scriptures;" says John's Jesus, "for in them ye think ye have eternal life: and they are they that testify of me" (John 5:39). Yes, the Hebrew scriptures, in the mind of this theologian, point to Jesus.

In 1935 the fragment called Papyrus Egerton 2 was discovered. It was the fragment of a lost gospel, known now as "the Unknown Gospel." Since this chapter has drawn on "lost Christianities" and has argued for an open canon, it is appropriate to let the Unknown Gospel have the last word over the relation between the Bible and Jesus Christ. Echoing John, this unknown writer records how Jesus "turned to the rulers of the people and spoke this word: 'Search the Scriptures, for you think that in them you have life. They are the ones that testify concerning me. Do not think that I came to accuse you to my Father. The one who accuses you is Moses, in whom you have hoped.' "[55]

8

On Not Being a "People of the Book"

We have found that appeal to the "plain sense" of the biblical text does *not* deliver plain answers. Indeed, the results of that appeal are a sufficient reason for abandoning the "guidebook approach" to the Bible. We also found that recent manuscript discoveries, comparative textual criticism, and church historical research strongly suggest a development at variance with official versions of the growth of the Catholic faith and its eventual canon. Conservative theology may choose to ignore these developments, much as it generally chooses to ignore the benefits to theology of the study of the sciences, or of those modern "masters of suspicion" in the social sciences, Marx, Durkheim, and Freud. A characteristic feature of conservative theology, Protestant and Catholic, consists in just this: ignore the inconvenient, and repeat the unlikely. Repetition is the chosen tactic of compliance and the assurance of certainty.

There is another type of biblicism which distinguishes itself from fundamentalism (and evangelicalism), and gives credence to the self-understanding of Christians as a "People of the Book."[1] This designation, shared with the other Semitic faiths, Judaism and Islam, may commendably increase the degree of rapport between individual adherents of these faiths. The designation is itself Islamic. *Sura* 29.45 of the Qur'an urges Muslims, "Do not dispute with the People of the Book: say, we believe in what has been sent down to us and what has been sent down to you; our God and your God is one." The term embraces the people of Judaism, Christianity, and Islam. It is a *Sura* that promises much by way of mutual inter-religious tolerance. Its danger lies in the implication that the relation between believers and their respective sacred texts lies along an axis of similarity. It is well known that fundamentalism, across the religions, thrives on "a theory of Scripture like the majority Islamic view of the Qur'an – as supernaturally inspired in origin, inerrant in content, and oracular in function."[2] What an irony that fundamentalist Christians who oppose Islam root and branch should share with them a near-identical theory of inspiration! Our worry, though, is less with fundamentalism, and more with the continuing seepage of biblicism into the mainstream of Christian theology.

Christian people are *not* the people of a book, even a very holy book. They are people of a Savior, the One who reveals a loving God who, by God's Spirit, remakes and renews humankind in the image of the Son. Christians do not have a written law and they are taught that they do not need one. Law-givers and prophets are not enough to bring about the transformation the world needs. The vision granted to Peter, James, and John at the "Transfiguration" (the incident where Jesus is seen transfigured, in the company of the law-giver Moses and the prophet Elijah) included the divine voice from a cloud telling them "This is my beloved Son: hear *him*" (Mark 9:7).[3] God comes among us as one of us. That is the qualitative distinction between the Christian faith and the other Semitic faiths without which no truthful conversation with them is possible and which the comparative study of holy books generally occludes. This last chapter criticizes the further elevation of the Bible in recent Protestant theology, suggests a way of disposing of the perennial problem of the Bible's authority, and proposes some principles for a peaceable reading of the Church's scriptures.

The Personalization of the Book

A good example of what I shall term "neo-biblicism" is the book *Holy Scripture: A Dogmatic Sketch*[4] by the distinguished theologian John Webster. It must be allowed to stand for a wide range of Reformed understandings of the Bible ("bibliology" is his preferred, neutral-sounding term). There is a promising start. "Holy Scripture," he says, is "the human text which God sanctifies for the service of his communicative presence."[5] The "witness" view of the Bible is confirmed, for theology is driven by the "belief in God's revelation as an event beyond all human history, to which Scripture bears witness and which finds confirmation in the Confessions of our Church."[6] So far, so good: "the Word made flesh and the scriptural word are in no way equivalent realities." Scripture is "holy" because through it we come to know God's saving acts. A crucial move is then made regarding how the Bible becomes holy. The term that the Church uses for the process of becoming holy is "sanctification," but this process is what happens to people. Webster acknowledges this, while subtly extending the term to the making holy of the Bible itself: "although the primary field in which the term is deployed remains that of the relation between divine and human persons, it may legitimately be extended to non-personal realities in so far as they are instruments of the personal relations between God and humankind."[7] The Bible, then, is "personalized." Its "holiness" is akin to the holiness of a holy person. To this point we shall soon need to return.

The work of sanctifying, of making holy, the Bible is minutely and definitively carried out by Godself in the Person of the Holy Spirit. It is said to be necessary for theology to offer "a theological description of the activity of God the Holy Spirit in sanctifying all the processes of the text's production, preservation and interpretation."[8] These are large claims indeed, and if they are successful, they provide a defense against the contingencies and vicissitudes discussed in the last chapter, including the differences between the manuscripts, the selection of appropriate books, and the right (and catholic) way of reading and expounding them. Now that the Bible is "personalized" (my term) the temptation becomes irresistible to invest the book with myriad personal qualities that normally belong to persons and their interactions.

There are several examples of the personalization of the Bible in *Holy Scripture*. In Christian theology the *Jews* are the elect or "chosen"

139

people of God, and their election is extended under the New Covenant to include the Gentiles. Well, God chooses writings as well as persons among what is elected, for if anything becomes holy, "it is by virtue of election, that is, by a sovereign act of segregation or separation by the Spirit as Lord."[9] The Bible is personalized because it is included in the personal category of what God elects. Or again, it is said that the Bible has a "servant-form."[10] It is "the sanctified servant of God in which the gospel is set before the attentive church."[11] Servants, however, are people too. Or again, as "pupils of scripture" (Calvin's term) we are "neither its masters nor its critics but learners in its school." That is a clear personalization. Again, summarizing part of Calvin's earlier Geneva **Catechism**, Webster says "the human reception of the Word" should be characterized by "submission, obedience and affection."[12] But these qualities belong of course to interactions between persons, and indicate the further extent to which the personalization of the book reaches in Protestant thought both early and late.

Which Comes First? The Bible or the Church?

A crucial issue for the Reformers lay, as we have seen, in the relation of Bible to Church. Webster's position on this is apparently clear. Both of them are the creation of the Word. Or, "the church is constituted by the Word, and by Holy Scripture as the Word's servant." The Bible is to be sharply differentiated from tradition, because scripture plays a role in the community of the Church that tradition doesn't. It mediates the divine presence and address unmistakably. "This, in the end, is why a strict demarcation between and ordering of Scripture and Tradition is required." "Accordingly, 'tradition' is best conceived of as a *hearing* of the Word rather than a fresh act of *speaking*."[13]

The Bible, then, has priority over tradition. Now that the strict demarcation between them has been made, the relation between the Bible and the Church can be theorized. The opposing positions are that the Bible is prior to the Church and judges it (Protestant); and that the Church is prior to the Bible and interprets it (Catholic). Webster subjugates Church and Bible to God the Word who creates them both and so is prior to each of them. "Scripture is not the word of the church; the church is the church of the Word." But the authority of the Bible in the Church has been a perennial and insuperable problem among conservatives, especially since they disagree about what it consists of and what follows from it. In *Holy Scripture*, the authority of the Bible is something acknowledged directly from reading it rather than something formally derived from it. "The authority of Scripture is its Spirit-bestowed capacity to quicken the church to truthful speech and righteous action" (another personalization?). We do not judge and interrogate the Bible. The Bible judges and interrogates us. The Holy Spirit does not merely animate the Church: the Spirit *commissions* the "apostolic testimony" that the Bible is. The Spirit enables the Church to recognize the books the Spirit inspires, for the Church's decisions about what should go in the Bible "are governed by the Holy Spirit who animates the church and enables its perception of the truth." When the Church decided what books were holy, it did so as "an act of faithful assent." The Holy Spirit told it! "Only in a secondary sense is canonisation an act of selection, authorisation or commendation on the church's part."[14]

Can anyone read the Bible rightly, discerningly? Well, there is a "true reader of Scripture" who needs a "correct attitude." "Rightly grasping the nature of Scripture involves both rational assent and a pious disposition of mind, will and affections." There is "faithful reading" to be done, and sin interferes with this. "Reading Scripture is thus a moral matter; it requires that we become certain kinds of readers, whose reading is taken up into the history of reconciliation." The test of historical-critical scholarship is whether it can "foster *childlike* reading of the text."[15]

The Personalistic Fallacy

Webster begins with the "witness view" of the Bible that is endorsed in this book. Clearly he is no fundamentalist, and his account of the Bible emphasizes its human, "creaturely" authors. His account is suffused with detailed knowledge of the Reformed tradition. On the one hand it is historically accurate and intellectually deft. On the other hand, it indicates the extent to which the Bible is over-valued in the Protestantism it represents, and the omission and perhaps willful neglect of the *consequences* of the over-valuation of the Bible make his analysis morally complacent (and even spiritually dangerous). Why, then, this seemingly harsh judgment?

First, there looms here the "personalistic fallacy" widespread in both moderate and extreme forms of Protestantism, introduced so naturally and inevitably that its lack of detection is almost a *fait accompli*. Biblical faith is faith in a God who "elects" a people as God's own, and through Christ God widens God's choice to include everyone. Indeed the whole creation is elected. This is a core belief of Christians, clearly endorsed by and derived from the Bible. But the Bible does not say that God elects it. How could it? Neither can the belief that God elects the Bible be derived from the doctrine of election because this doctrine is about something else and ought not to be annexed in this way. But there are stronger versions of the personalistic fallacy which play a more important part in transforming the Bible into something else. The Gospels indicate that high on the list of titles and roles that early Christian faith assigned to Jesus is that he is God's Servant: "The Son of Man did not come to be served, but to serve, and to give his life as a ransom for many" (Mark 10:45[16]). The humility of a servant is a mark of the Christian life, (e.g., Mark 10:44) in the name of the One who "took upon him the form of a servant" (Philippians 2:7). *Jesus*, for Christians, is the Suffering Servant of God announced in Isaiah 53. *It is the Christ, not the Bible, that has the form of a servant*; Christ, who is "the sanctified servant of God." The displacement of Christ and the elevation of the Book lurk in Webster's characterizations.

The same judgment is invited with regard to the idea of the Bible as a school and as that to which obedience is required. There are plenty of Bible schools in the world, but the Bible *as* a school? Is that not an obvious category mistake, unmitigated by its pious intention? While the servant personalization displaces the Son, the school personalization displaces the Holy Spirit for, according to John's Jesus, it is the

142

Spirit, not the Bible, that is the Church's guide: "When he, the Spirit of truth, is come, he will guide you into all truth: for he shall not speak of himself; but whatsoever he shall hear, that shall he speak: and he will shew you things to come" (John 16:13). It might even be plausibly suggested that the attitude required of pupils in the school of scripture displaces God the Father. Thankfully there are several ways of unpacking what human obedience to God amounts to without buying into the usual passivities and hierarchies that obedience is generally thought to require. Obeying God always or nearly always requires mediation through someone else – the priest, the slavemaster, the televangelist, the abuser. So much for childlike readings of texts. The Bible itself contains a case where a Gentile, an African government official, was reading Isaiah (53:7–8) and making no sense of it (Acts 8:26–40). Clearly he was learning nothing in the school of scripture. Neither does the process whereby the official comes to understand this passage as referring to Jesus Christ conform to cozy assumptions about the Spirit showing us what it means. Yes, there is a reference to the Holy Spirit in the account of this incident, notable especially for what the Spirit does *not* do. The Spirit does not directly illumine the prepared heart of this inquiring man. The Spirit tells Philip to meet the official and *tell* him what the passage means, because without someone to explain it, it never will be understood: "Understandest thou what thou readest? And he said, How can I, except some man should guide me?" (Acts 8:30–1). If we are to understand ancient scriptures we need interpretation, and for interpretation we require interpreters, however much they may hide themselves in dogmas about the plain sense of scripture addressing us.

The personalistic fallacy is widespread in contemporary Protestantism. Ellen Davis and Richard Hays, for example, wisely instructing Bible readers to deploy their imaginations when engaging with the imaginative acts of God to be found there, remark "If we are faithful readers of the stories of these imaginative acts, we will find our own imaginations expanded and transformed. *Scripture will claim us and make us into new people.*"[17] What? *Scripture* will claim us? Not the risen Lord or the Spirit's illumination? Who wants to be claimed by a book? Indeed there are Bible passages that warn against this idolatry. Even if this is a careless figure of speech it reveals the near-omnipresence of the personalistic fallacy, insisting that we surrender to the Bible, listen to the Bible, be judged by the Bible instead of surrendering to God. "The Scriptures are our guide, and we, their apprentices. This conviction ought readily to be embraced by all Christians."[18] Here is the guidebook view again (and the pupil metaphor), trotted out as obligatory and self-evident. Again no thought has been given to the disastrous consequences that this unguarded veneration of scripture has elicited in the history of Bible use.

Another blatant example of the personalistic fallacy is the very title of Walter Brueggemann's book, *The Book That Breathes New Life*. Brueggemann is a deservedly popular theologian (and I agree with much of his work). Has he considered, I wonder, whether the title of this mainstream work borders on the blasphemous? In Christianity it is the *Holy Spirit* who breathes new life, not the inanimate book! Christ offers new life, not some text! Over the "issue of the authority of the Bible" Brueggemann says he is one of "those of us who claim and intend to stake our lives on its attestation."[19] But that remark only belies his desperation. Why not stake his life on Christ instead, for which he knows there is much biblical warrant? Why not abandon this **foundational** quest, especially as he admits the question will "remain endlessly unsettled and … perpetually disputatious." He offers his personal reflection on "how it is that I work with, relate to, and submit to the Bible." But why submit to the Bible? Would it not be more biblical (and much safer) to submit to Christ instead? If we submit to anyone should it not be to God alone?

Hundreds of Protestant theologians have convinced themselves that when they read the Bible, it speaks to them. The Bible, they confidently assert, "speaks": it "says," while we "listen" and of course "obey." It is necessary to point to an obvious fact – that "speaks" is a metaphor – in order to unmask the dangerous and potentially disastrous category mistake that these loose **locutionary** metaphors appear to authorize. Texts do not speak. They let themselves be read. What

144

I have been calling the "personalistic fallacy" Dale Martin calls "the myth of textual agency," a myth so deeply embedded in the religious consciousness that he has devoted much of his writing to "disabuse" people of it.[20] Since the ascription of agency is one (limited) way of describing what a person is, the myth of textual agency and the personalistic fallacy are similar expressions, doing similar jobs and exercising similar suspicions regarding the hidden procedures and destructive consequences that accompany the use of each. In particular, Martin uncovers the dishonesty of this sort of biblical exegesis. The people who say "the Bible says," he says, "never admit that the Bible doesn't actually talk. They do not acknowledge their own interpretive practices by which they have arrived at what they think the Bible 'says.'" He too thinks that "People throughout history, therefore, have committed grave ethical offenses – supporting slavery, oppressing women, fighting unjust wars, killing, torturing, and harming their fellow human beings – under cover of 'the Bible says.'"[21] Exactly. That is all too often the consequence of the obsequious veneration of the Bible advocated by Webster and too many of his contemporaries. These "interpretive practices" are idolatrous. That is why their consequences are so often violent. Perhaps that is why their guardians need to keep them concealed? Idolatry really *is* sin, especially when the Bible is its object of worship.

"Dis-solving" the Problem of Authority

I think the personalistic fallacy reaches into the very engine room of idolatry. It indicates how bibliolatry gets manufactured and then cloaked with piety, often mellifluous in its expression. Devotion to the Book may become as intense as devotion to a particular person or to God. Webster says a "strict demarcation between and ordering of Scripture and Tradition is required." But why is it required? The answer is that Webster's "bibliology" requires it. Nothing in fact or history requires it. Indeed the facts blur the demarcation between the two, for the New Testament books themselves once were called tradition. Once the Bible is loaded up with **ontological** freight, and made into something that it isn't, absolute distinctions are needed between what texts (in their original versions?) are genuinely inspired, or elected by the Holy Spirit into the canon, and what texts are not, so that these 39, or these 27, or these 66 books, or however many the Holy Spirit elects, are exclusively Holy Scripture, while no other books are. The fallibility which Webster is content to ascribe to the human authors of the books cannot be extended to the decisions of the Councils about which books are inspired. But the theory drives the facts. Scripture must be contained, defined, and enclosed if it, and no other texts, is to have the properties it is alleged to have. There remains an alternative view, of course – that the formation of the canon was never finalized (see chapter 7 above) *as the Reformers themselves had begun to acknowledge*, and so its boundaries must therefore remain doubtful and open. Were those Christians who had doubts about Jude and Revelation not inspired too? Who is to say they were not?

The authority of the Bible in the Church is a perennial problem. I think the problem is acute because the Church, especially the Protestant branches of it, has made persistently exaggerated claims for the Bible that cannot be sustained, and has thereby generated for itself an endless search for a foundationalism of the Book that cannot succeed because the claims it makes cannot be warranted. But neither are they needed. The prospects for Webster's answer are not bright either. "The authority of Scripture is its Spirit-bestowed capacity to quicken the church to truthful speech and righteous action." Really? So when the Church used its savage texts to persecute, ostracize, burn, and exile defenseless people, was this "Spirit-bestowed"? What checks are in place to ensure that the present homophobic readings of the Bible that fuel the persecution of lesbian and gay Christians are "Spirit-filled"? Is their constant exclusion and problematization by evangelical Christians "righteous action"? Is this "capacity to quicken" a property of the Bible, or its godly readers, or the Spirit? The shifting of the problem of the authority of the Bible from the status of the Bible in the Church to the Bible's ability to inspire Christians to

146

righteous actions evades the difficulties of the prior formulation, and is actually harmful in its unintended effects. It is morally indifferent to what it authorizes.

So the problem of the authority of the Bible is resolved in part by what the Church does when it reads it. We are currently witnessing savage, shameful readings of the Bible, all of them girded with the alleged finality and justifying power of some theory of biblical authority. It is a common solution. Brueggemann attempts it too. First there is a verbal slide from the difficult question of the authority of the Bible to something more manageable, the question of *authorization*: "Authority has to do with *issues of authorization*, that is, how, in a pluralistic world like ours, concrete communities can be authorized to live, act, and hope in a manner that may at times oppose the accepted norm, a manner that can be justified neither scientifically nor experientially."[22] Or again, "The authority of scripture must ultimately be articulated in confessional terms by communities that assert that they have discerned the truth of power and the power of truth precisely in this text." This "confessional claim" he continues, "is what is meant by the 'self-authenticating authority of Scripture.'" The Bible, then, is able to authorize the *practice* of churches because it has the "potential to release from false notions of absoluteness and certitude, and to unite a community currently beset by partisan and divisive pluralism."[23] This is what enables belief in biblical authority to be sustained.

Brueggemann is wisely steering his readers away from sterile questions about the Bible's authority towards fertile questions about what the Bible authorizes, but if he is hoping to arrive at some new foundational basis for maintaining the excessive veneration of the Bible in right-wing Protestantism, he is certain to disappoint. Opponents will readily point out that he conflates the authority of the Bible with how communities of Bible readers behave. But that is a shift of emphasis that soon withers with embarrassment. Apart from that, this new basis for thinking about authority collapses for other reasons. First, it is not just the Bible that influences churches. If they are to be faithful Christians, they will need to draw on other sources through which the Word of God is present, and through which the Spirit breathes, such as Christian doctrine, the Creeds, the Wisdom that courses through creation, the spiritual nurture that the Eucharist provides, and God's partial disclosure through tradition, reason, experience, and so on. This "Bible **positivism**" is another example of *sola scriptura*, as if nothing else were pertinent. Second, the appeal to the self-authentication or self-interpretation of the Bible is likely to be, finally, incoherent. In ordinary parlance, to authenticate a claim about something, say an insurance claim in the event of an accident, or the age and value of an antique object, or the genuineness of a passport, and so on, necessarily requires reference to something beyond or outside what is authenticated if it is to succeed. Can anything authenticate *itself*? Brueggemann seems to understand this by locating the authority of the Bible outside itself and inside what Christian communities do with it. But what they do with it is just the problem that modern hermeneutics finds too hot to handle. And which communities? The idea of a "community" of readers is vacuously open-ended. Are the Episcopalians, or the Old Catholics, or the Mormons "communities"? Or local branches of each? Thirdly (and sadly), while the Bible has the "potential to release from false notions of absoluteness and certitude," it also has the potential to release outbursts of savagery, hatred, and religious arrogance, and to *create* false notions of absoluteness and certitude. How does the Bible unite a community? Has Brueggemann not noticed that the communities that appeal most to the Bible are the ones that are most divided?

David Ford tries to include Christian wisdom in his "wisdom interpretation of scripture."[24] He links wisdom ingeniously to *crying*: chapter 1 is entitled "Wisdom Cries." Drawing on Luke's Gospel, he finds cries of amazement, and of "blessing, praise, thanks, complaint, repentance, petition and sheer joy."[25] Cries are "a sign of the limits of speech," and when we get to that point we may address, or be addressed by, the transcendent God. Alongside cries of praise are the cries of the suffering, including the loud cry of Christ suffering on the cross. Ford says, "*If Jesus embodies wisdom, then wisdom is vitally concerned to hear and respond with compassion to the cries of those who are suffering.*"[26] These are themselves wise words, but two caveats are needed before following Ford entirely. Ford finds the cry of wisdom in the scriptures he chooses. What is the relation between the cries we find in the Bible and the cries of people suffering and rejoicing now? Discerning wisdom in contemporary life, as well as in ancient texts, is the urgent task. Secondly, in this book we have concentrated on the cries of victims of the savage text, whose agonies past and present cry out to be understood as the protest of divine wisdom against persecuting biblicism. A "wisdom interpretation" of these cries is essential for a more adequate understanding of what the Bible is and how it should be used.

There is another way of dealing with the problem of the authority of the Bible. Theology can borrow the method of problem-solving that the philosopher Wittgenstein used in relation to problems in philosophy. Wittgenstein did not look for solutions to problems, but for *dis*solutions. He wrote, "A philosophical problem has the form, 'I don't know my way about.'"[27] Traditional problems about mind, language, consciousness, being, could, he thought, be eased by showing that they were based on prior mistakes, mistakes which ignored contexts, or which made category errors, or failed to appreciate the complexity of actual language use and so on. I think the theological problem of the authority of the Bible can be "dis-solved" in a similar way. Once the Bible is separated out from tradition, made into a guidebook, treated as a person, and appealed to exclusively, its authority is bound to become a problem giving rise to battles against scientists, social scientists, theologians, philosophers, historians, other Christians – anyone who appears to threaten it. Once the Bible is treated as divinely authored, of course its authority becomes a problem, like its relationship to other sources of revelation. But treat the New Testament as a series of documents of the earliest Church, witnessing to Jesus and to what God had done through him; acknowledge the Bible as the primary tradition of the Church alongside the secondary tradition that extends to the present, and the problem of authority is dissolved. Christians find God in the Bible when they look beyond its pages to the divine Word, in whom "was life; and the life was the light of men"

(John 1:4). These scriptures are the Church's scriptures. What could be simpler? The Church uses them when it summons people to the faith it upholds, and when it nurtures itself in that faith. They are the primary documents of the faith for Christians. They have, and always will have, pre-eminence over others.

Reading these scriptures also invites the response that there are sources of revelation outside them which can no longer be ignored. Christians can claim the Bible to confirm their identity as followers of the Christ. Indeed they can truthfully say the Bible is indispensable for this task. That doesn't seem problematic at all. The problem for people outside the faith lies where it always did: whether Jesus is Lord and whether the faith is true. There is no need to compound that problem with another one: about the inspiration of the Bible, or its divine authority, or the impossibility of it being wrong in matters of spiritual importance, or of it possessing some bibliological property that guarantees its supernatural ability to impress. Paul could not have made the point more tellingly when he observed: "For other foundation can no man lay than that is laid, which is Jesus Christ" (1 Corinthians 3:11).

Appeals to "the true reader of Scripture" and to "faithful reading" complacently beg questions. Which readings are faithful? Webster's? Those of the Kirk which did not suffer a witch to live? They were pious, faithful people, truly devout. Reading *Holy Scripture* one could not guess that there were scores of "**texts of terror**" in the pages of the Bible. Presumably all of those considered in part II must be received with due gratitude, humility, and docility? May we not find the prompting of God's Spirit precisely in that holy sense of resistance to these texts, or in the moral disbelief that they engender deep within the souls of readers? Apparently they are not even a problem worthy of a footnote.

Must we not be at least suspicious of the assertion that the Holy Spirit brings about the gift of the canon to the Church? Are not the textual and historical difficulties raised in chapter 7 genuine difficulties in the face of believing this? Presumably there must be some sort of match between theory and history at this point; otherwise it must remain dogma (in the worst sense). Webster makes the familiar "strict demarcation" between the Bible and tradition and affirms the priority of the former over the latter. This demarcation is spectacularly successful in much Protestant thought. It licenses an **intuitionism** of reading which lures Bible readers into thinking a direct reading of the Bible is possible which bypasses the history of its reception. It allows an unrestrained individualism of interpretation to occur and devalues tradition.[28]

My worries extend of course beyond Webster's robust bibliology to the equal veneration of texts that inspire savagery, and texts that witness to Jesus Christ. Two further matters must be added before suggesting an alternative way of proceeding. There is enormous diversity in the Bible, not simply of different literary genres, but of religious content. This diversity embraces differences between the synoptic Gospels and the Gospel of John; the different theologies and styles of Paul and James, of Paul and the later writings that bear his name, between Gospel and Apocalypse, and so on. That lively diversity is part of the attractiveness of Bible reading. Interpretation of the Bible has concentrated mainly on its unity rather than its diversity. But this leads to a further sense of the uniformity of text, whereas the recognition of diversity allows more readily the sense of gradation of worth that what is preserved in the Bible actually has (for example, a preference for the Love Commandments of the Gospels over the insults to women in the **Pastoral Letters**). I prefer the plural term used by Jesus when he spoke about the Hebrew scriptures, *hai graphai*, or "the writings." The singular (capitalized) term "Scripture," increasingly common in conservative writing, may perhaps be chosen deliberately because of the homogeneous (and misleading) impression it gives that within this single category all is equally capable of being used by the Spirit to inspire the Church. The heterogeneous (and biblical) plural "scriptures" is more satisfactory. (The singular "Bible" also conveys a sense of homogeneity unavailable from the plural Greek word *biblia*, "little books," from which it derives.)

Second I wish, after a century of ecumenism, that Protestant and Catholic accounts of what the Bible is might move both towards each other, and on. The Council of Trent reacted highly defensively to the irruption of Protestantism, while Protestantism, having become established as a series of new churches, piled up endless justifications for its biblicism and its pretence that tradition can be bypassed in its encounter with God's Word. The Vatican seems determined not to be outdone by the Protestant emphasis on the Bible, so instead of learning from Protestant biblicism, it reaffirms its earlier position instead of developing it imaginatively and congruently with the contributions of hundreds of Roman Catholic scholars. Protestants and Catholics need one another! As Christopher Evans remarked nearly 40 years ago, "the Reformation was nowhere more disastrous than in its belief that it had achieved a fixed doctrine of the position of scripture in the church."[29] Bible-centered Christianity reinvents itself, often in dangerous forms, and the excess weight it gives to its Holy Book can be explained by the removal of so much else, at the time of the Reformation and subsequently.

Some Principles for a Peaceful Reading of the Bible

How, then, might the Bible be read in a way that enables readers to be faithful to God's revelation in Christ while avoiding present and future catastrophes of interpretation?

The Need for Principles

In the first instance there is a need to create a set of principles governing our Bible use which is itself *holy*, that is, which enables the possibility that God might inspire our reading, and hearers of the Church's proclamation might recognize its divine origin. Since the need for principles and their identification are separate matters, let us take each in turn.

I have found, when writing as a Christian theologian about families, or marriage, or sexuality, that I have drawn extensively and thankfully from the Bible. Such writing would have been impossible otherwise. However, I have also found it necessary to state clearly how I was using the Bible in these writings. I have thought it was particularly necessary to reassure readers skeptical of confronting *any* writing that tells them what the Bible says, or that claims to base itself on "biblical teaching," that they were not being preached to, or taken for a ride. Indeed they were being offered arguments, based on consistent principles, which were intended to persuade readers of the truth of their conclusions.[30] In fact almost everyone who wants to use the Bible to inspire, or persuade, or suggest is required to do this if s/he wants to be taken seriously.

Isaac Newton (1642–1727), the famous English mathematician and physicist, devised 15 "Rules for interpreting the words and language in Scripture."[31] Charles Cosgrove's *Appealing to Scripture in Moral Debate* devises "five hermeneutical rules" (the book's subtitle) which he makes explicit from "the *tacit* hermeneutical assumptions at work in appeal to the Bible as scripture."[32] Where Cosgrove has five rules, *The Art of Reading Scripture* project painstakingly enounces nine theses, all of which are to be taken as true, and marshaled together in order to perform the activity of faithful interpretation of the Bible.[33] Keith Ward enunciates "six principles of biblical interpretation."[34] These authors and many more honestly recognize the problematic nature of their primary source, while remaining determined to use it constructively. The final task of this volume is to suggest principles which will help to promote peaceable and faithful Bible reading and avoid the textual savagery that has disfigured the preaching of the Gospel past and present. The principles are not exhaustive. They overlap with each other, and with the similar efforts of similar authors.

1   *Read the Bible to learn of God's Word*

The first principle must be that Christians read the Bible in order to learn about God's Word, that is, God's self-communication in Christ to which the Bible bears witness. Keith Ward puts it simply: "The Bible gives us its own main principle of interpretation when it tells us that the love of God in Jesus is the culminating point of its teaching.

153

Only when we keep that firmly in mind can we be sure of being true to what the Bible really teaches."[35]

This principle has been kept to the fore during the writing of this book. We have seen how one very like it was required of African American Christians in the USA in the nineteenth and twentieth centuries. Renita Weems, summarizing the handling of the Bible among them, observed that "it is not texts per se that function authoritatively. Rather, it is reading strategies, and more precisely, *particular* readings that turn out, in fact, to be authoritative."[36] There are two obvious points to be made about Bible reading among newly literate slaves. They were suspicious of the slavemasters' interpretation of it, so "even if one concedes that the Bible is authoritative, one still has not said anything about how the Bible should be interpreted." And greeted with the polyphony of Protestant voices all speaking from the Bible, they knew they could rely on none of them. "After all, the history of Protestantism aptly points out that different readings (and hence interpretations) of the one fixed text, the Bible, have existed simultaneously."[37] Instead they needed a hermeneutic that revealed God's great love for them in such a way that liberation from slavery was a consequence of it. They knew that Eurocentric exegesis could not speak to them in their condition, and they developed reading strategies for dealing with that.

This principle would have been endorsed by Luther. As Karl Barth reminds us, "The well-known criterion of Luther was to test every Scripture by whether 'it sets forth Christ or not.' 'What teacheth not Christ is not apostolic, even though Peter or Paul teacheth it. Again what preacheth Christ is apostolic, even though Judas, Annas, Pilate and Herod doth it' (*Preface to the Epistles of St. James and St. Jude*, 1522)."[38] But testing scripture is a very different activity from obeying it; indeed it could be seen as the original hermeneutic of suspicion, for without the prior doubt that it may set forth many other things apart from Christ, there would be no need to test it at all. Here Luther is unlike many of his evangelical successors.

He is also unlike them with regard to the meaning of that **polysemic** term "Word of God." It should not be assumed that Luther thought that the Bible was straightforwardly the Word of God. The distinguished editor of Luther's works in English, Jaroslav Pelikan, explains that Luther understood the Word of God "as the concrete action of God. The concrete things of the created world were all words of God, because each of them owed its existence to God's creating deed."[39] Luther thought that, "When God spoke his Word in Christ, He did so through both words and deeds." Luther enjoyed pointing out that "Christ Himself did not write anything; but He spoke and preached continually, to make it clear that the basic form of the Word of God was always the oral Word of proclamation." While preaching remains popular among evangelical Christians, it is doubtful whether the basic form of the Word among many of them is the oral, rather than the written Word! The idea that Luther meant the Bible by "Word of God" is a "caricature." (That said, Pelikan admits that "Most of the time Luther, like the Scriptures themselves, did not mean the scriptures when he spoke about the "Word of God." But sometimes *he did.*")[40]

Luther, then, placed the Word of God who was Christ before the Word of God which is the Bible. It is a striking confirmation of what has been called here "the witness view of the Bible." We can affirm this principle without reducing God's self-communication to Christ alone. But even among writers who admit the need for principles of interpretation, there is a lack of appreciation of this qualitative distinction. Brueggemann wants to detach the Bible from Jesus and to make it an independent revelation. "The purpose and effect of scripture in the Christian faith community is that it is 'revelatory,' that is, it is in its very character a 'revelation.'"[41] One wishes for a greater emphasis on Jesus Christ being the revelation the Bible shows us. Cosgrove's work on Bible use says nothing directly about what the Bible is for or why Christians read it. There is nothing about Jesus in the five rules. One of these, the Rule of Analogy,[42] seems to validate the bypassing of both Christ and tradition in Bible reading. By positing similarities (analogies) between biblical times and our own, all inconvenient discontinuity in time between the two periods is removed and we can find ourselves in comfortingly close company with apostles and prophets.

155

2   *Expect moral and spiritual development in the Bible*

The Bible is always surpassing itself, and this is evidence for the growing spiritual illumination of its authors, reversing and cancelling the limited wisdom of earlier generations. Here are two examples. In Deuteronomy there is a prohibition against illegitimate men and men with incomplete or damaged sexual organs being part of "the congregation of the Lord." "He that is wounded in the stones, or hath his privy member cut off, shall not enter into the congregation of the Lord. A bastard shall not enter … even to his tenth generation" (23:1–2). The writer of Isaiah 56 understands the sheer moral awfulness of this. As if to compensate for their exclusion he says, "neither let the eunuch say, Behold I am a dry tree. For thus saith the Lord unto the eunuchs that keep my sabbaths … Even unto them will I give in mine house and within my walls a place and a name better than of sons and of daughters" (Isaiah 56:3–5). The third of the Ten Commandments (or the second, depending on your preferred arithmetic) contains a vicious warning about the punitive consequences of idol worship: "Thou shalt not bow down thyself to them, nor serve them: for I the LORD thy God am a jealous God, visiting the iniquity of the fathers upon the children unto the third and fourth generation of them that hate me" (Exodus 20:5). Both Jeremiah and Ezekiel repudiate this savagery: "In those days they shall say no more, The fathers have eaten a sour grape, and the children's teeth are set on edge. But every one shall die for his own iniquity: every man that eateth the sour grape, his teeth shall be set on edge" (Jeremiah 31:29–30; see Ezekiel 18:2–3, 20). Jeremiah looked towards a "new covenant" with the "house of Israel" which Christians identify with themselves. However, even if this identification is not pressed, Jeremiah's words are testimony to his conviction of the inadequacy of the Mosaic law and the need for it to be surpassed. The implication is unavoidable. Faithfulness to God, openness to new inspiration, requires some negation of what has been revealed before.

Keith Ward calls this "the principle of sublation." He says "sublate" means "to negate and yet to fulfil at the same time."[43] Ward's examples take him to the Sermon on the Mount, where Jesus says "Think not that I am come to destroy the law, or the prophets: I am not come to destroy, but to fulfil" (Matthew 5:17). The rest of Matthew 5 is taken up with six units of the teaching of Jesus (on murder, adultery, divorce, oath-taking, retaliation, and neighbor love), which use the approximate formula "Ye have heard that it was said by them of old time … But I say unto you …" (Matthew 5:21–2). Each of these shows what the fulfillment of the law and the prophets means and requires. The teaching of "them of old time" is not "destroyed," for it is fulfilled in what replaces it. But in each case the new teaching inserts a qualitative difference between itself and its replacement. Take for example the fulfillment of the command to love one's neighbor by widening it in order to include one's enemy:

> Ye have heard that it hath been said, Thou shalt love thy neighbour, and hate thine enemy. But I say unto you, Love your enemies, bless them that curse you, do good to them that hate you, and pray for them which despitefully use you, and persecute you; That ye may be the children of your Father which is in heaven: for he maketh his sun to rise on the evil and on the good, and sendeth rain on the just and on the unjust. (Matthew 5:43–5)

These are obvious, in fact spectacular, cases of sublation. Matthew intends to ram home the contrast between the teaching of the **Torah** and the teaching of Jesus Christ. These cases are also dramatic because the contrast is not simply between one Bible passage and another, but between the teaching of Jesus and what "was said by them of old time." Sublation is a term that *allows* that contrast to be spectacular because it allows what was once accepted as God's "Word" to be negated by the greater revelation that surpasses it. That is why Ward says "The Bible is filled with sublations, which means that many biblical passages, taken in their straightforward sense, must now be accounted false. It is a vital principle of biblical interpretation that we gradually learn to discern when and in what way specific biblical texts are to be sublated by others."

157

3   Read the Old Testament through the New Testament

It is tempting to say that the Old Testament is sublated by the New, but this would be difficult to claim without risking further anti-Semitism. Jesus himself taught that on the two commandments to love God and one's neighbor "hang all the law and the prophets" (Matthew 22:40). But even these two commandments are directly based on the law (Deuteronomy 6:5 and Leviticus 19:18). Jews remain the neighbors of Christians, in fact closer to them than adherents of other faiths. Jesus, the apostles, and the early disciples were all practicing Jews, and the Hebrew scriptures were also the scriptures of the earliest churches (see chapter 6 above).

The principle "Read the Old Testament through the New Testament" allows priority to be given to the New, as the fulfillment of the Old. The author of Hebrews clearly thinks that Christ sublates the Hebrew prophets: "God, who at sundry times and in divers manners spake in time past unto the fathers by the prophets, Hath in these last days spoken unto us by his Son, whom he hath appointed heir of all things, by whom also he made the worlds" (Hebrews 1:1–2). This author is clear that, at the very least, the new covenant supersedes the old. Commenting on Jeremiah's prophecy of a new covenant he remarks: "In that he saith, A new covenant, he hath made the first old. Now that which decayeth and waxeth old is ready to vanish away" (Hebrews 8:13). On the other hand, Paul uses a horticultural metaphor to explain how the new covenant is based on the old. The old covenant is like an olive tree. Some of its branches were broken off, and a "wild olive tree" grafted on. But the old tree and its roots continue to give life to the new one (Romans 11:16–24).

The basic ethnic distinction in the New Testament is between Jews and non-Jews (Gentiles). Once the Jews alone were the chosen people of God. Now all people are the people of God. The Gentiles have arrived. The status of the Jewish people as God's chosen is unaffected by this Good News. The scriptures which Christians have traditionally called the "Old Testament" are read differently by Jews. If Christians cannot believe in the new covenant that God has made with all creation, then the Messiah has not come. What matters of course, is not whether Christian identity is **supercessionist** but whether it is anti-Semitic; whether Christians in affirming their different religious identity can do so without harming the religious integrity of the Jewish people and without allowing their differences to erupt into yet more violence against them.

Christians can treat the Old Testament now much as the first Christians treated it then. And that was variously![44] It is hard to see how Christians can agree with the arguments of Paul in Romans about the connection between the law of the Old Testament and the consciousness of sin, which Christ removes, and not accept the principle of sublation in some form when reading them. Yet, without the Old Testament, Christian confidence in the doctrine of creation, or its prophetic understanding of social justice, or its grasp of the omnipresence of divine Wisdom in the world, would all be greatly stunted. The fulfillment of the Hebrew scriptures in Christ does not mean that Christians read their own scriptures aright (we have seen that many do not) or that Jews do not. It does mean that Christians read the Old Testament in a particular way that allows the New Testament priority.

At the beginning of the second century the letters of Clement (dated 80–140 CE) and Ignatius (who died between 98 and 117 CE) illustrate a polarization of the problem. For Clement "scripture is the Old Testament. His letter is to a considerable extent made up of quotation from it, and he can settle the main questions, including the ministry with which he is principally concerned, by reference to it."[45] Well before the formation of the New Testament canon, Ignatius, bishop of Antioch, dealt, in his letter to the Philadelphians, with the problem of the relation between the life of Jesus Christ and the scriptures (the Old Testament) that pointed to him. Ignatius describes the controversy like this: "When I heard some saying, If I do not find it in the ancient Scriptures, I will not believe the Gospel; on my saying to them, It is written, they answered me, That remains to be proved." The question at issue of course is what *is* written, and Ignatius' answer is clear, "But to me Jesus Christ is in the place of all that is ancient: His cross, and death, and resurrection, and the faith which is by Him, are undefiled monuments of antiquity."[46] At the same time Christians needed the Jewish scriptures. How else could they know who Jesus was? "[W]ithout the Jewish scriptures, Christians lacked the one thing they needed for religious legitimacy in the ancient world: a claim to antiquity."[47]

4   Read the Bible through the Rule

The Bible should be interpreted through the "**rule of faith**" or through the principal creeds of the Church. Tertullian (155–230 CE) dealt with the problem of the use of scripture in combating heresy. His answer was *not* to use the scriptures (we cannot yet say "the Bible"), not even to discuss them, with heretics. Arguing on the basis of the scriptures, he taught, produces "no other effect than help to upset either the stomach or the brain."[48] He was exasperated at the futility of arguing on the basis of scriptural passages against opponents who read them differently or appealed to different passages in support of their opposing views. That was Hooker's view. It is a circle of futility well known today. "Though most skilled in the Scriptures, you will make no progress, when everything which you maintain is denied on the other side, and whatever you deny is (by them) maintained. As for yourself, indeed, you will lose nothing but your breath, and gain nothing but vexation from their blasphemy."

How is truth to be discerned, then, unless by the scriptures? Tertullian's answer was to appeal to who Christ was in his very being, in his teaching, and in the Catholic faith and order which had been handed down and received. "Our appeal," he averred, "must not be made to the Scriptures." Rather there is a prior question, indeed "the only one which we must discuss: 'With whom lies that very faith to which the Scriptures belong. From what and through whom, and when, and to whom, has been handed down that rule, by which men become Christians?'" "For wherever it shall be manifest that the true Christian rule and faith shall be, *there* will likewise be the true Scriptures and expositions thereof, and all the Christian traditions." Christ declared everything about himself and his teaching, entrusted it to the apostles, who preached it throughout the world, "founded

160

churches in every city, from which all the other churches, one after another, derived the tradition of the faith, and the seeds of doctrine, and are every day deriving them, that they may become churches."[49]

I have lingered with Ignatius and Tertullian because they have much to teach us about handling the Bible in contemporary arguments today. What matters most is the Church's confession that Jesus Christ is truly human, truly God, and that, as the Athanasian Creed says, "The Catholick faith is this: That we worship one God in Trinity and Trinity in unity." The Bible does not directly say these things. Tradition does. The Creeds express the faith of the Church, albeit in a historically relative way. "In a fundamental sense the creed is simply the way the church reads scripture."[50] Jesus Christ is "what is written." Tertullian discovered the uselessness of the direct appeal to scriptures. It bypassed the Church, as it bypassed tradition. It was bound to be inconclusive. Conducting theological disputes in this way, he also thought, conceded legitimacy to poor arguments and deficient exegesis (as it still does), thereby encouraging the very sentiments to which the Catholic faith was opposed. But his solution cannot finally be ours, not least because a better way of treating heretics is to learn to love them and to thank God for the partial grasp of the truth which they already possess. Unfortunately, the proposition "wherever it shall be manifest that the true Christian rule and faith shall be, *there* will likewise be the true Scriptures and expositions thereof, and all the Christian traditions," begs questions. To *whom* is it manifest? The powerful? We have already noted that the growth of early Christianity and the growth of the Catholic tradition are far from coterminous. Luther's break with Rome arose because he denied that the Catholic tradition provided "true Christian rule and faith" or true exposition of the scriptures. The argument here does not adjudicate that perilous quarrel. Our conclusion is more modest: that Tertullian was right to refuse to argue as later generations did, *sola scriptura*. The Bible must be read through the Church's understanding of it, and that understanding is theological and creedal.

Robert Jenson has succinctly stated what the Bible is *for*. The Church "gathered these documents for her specific purpose: to aid in preserving her peculiar message, to aid in maintaining across time, from the apostles to the End, the self-identity of her message that the God of Israel has raised his servant Jesus from the dead."[51] From this simple position he urges a simple "hermeneutical exhortation" upon his readers: "Be entirely blatant and unabashed in reading Scripture for the church's purposes, and within the context of Christian faith and practice. Indeed, *guide your reading by church doctrine*."[52] In other words, "Read the Bible through the Rule!"

5   *Make the Love Commandments the guide to ethical practice*

The Love Commandments of Jesus *are* Christian ethical teaching and practice. The outworking of these is the fulfillment of the law (Matthew 22:40), and the ethical practice of the Church needs continuous revision in the light of them. These commands are the "guide" to the treatment of the Other, and to negotiating difference. They also need to be set against reductionistic accounts which do not do justice to the rich moral vision to which these commandments belong. As Pope Benedict XVI has said,

> The transition which he [Jesus] makes from the Law and the Prophets to the twofold commandment of love of God and of neighbour, and his grounding the whole life of faith on this central precept, is not simply a matter of morality – something that could exist apart from and alongside faith in Christ and its sacramental re-actualization. Faith, worship and ethos are interwoven as a single reality which takes shape in our encounter with God's agape.[53]

The practice of Christian love is a sharing in God's own nature, that which was revealed in the self-giving of God in Christ upon the cross. That practice is renewed in the Eucharist. "If ye keep my commandments, ye shall abide in my love; even as I have kept my Father's commandments, and abide in his love." (John 15:10) The process of "abiding" in love is nothing less than a mystical participation in the Love that God is. This is a qualitatively different experience from that of obedience to a Supernatural Being whose commands we are required to obey: it is rather a being taken over by the Love that reconciles all things to Itself, and that goes on forgiving and reconciling. This is also qualitatively different from "situation ethics," a theory popular in the 1960s according to which one was supposed to intuit the demand of love in every situation. That was secular intuitionism, commandeered by liberal theology. "Abiding" in God is instead the fullness of Christian life and worship. Everyone knows that "love" is fraught with many meanings. Christians build their understanding of love from the self-giving of God in Christ.

6 Treat the Bible as Primary Tradition

Protestant Churches need to learn more from their own recent tradition of historical criticism and from the Catholics' valuing of tradition: Roman Catholics need to learn from historical criticism and to apply this to tradition too. There is much in official Catholic teaching about the Bible that accords with the argument of this book, and some that is contrary to it. Official teaching on divine revelation maintains the distinction between Word and words. Christ is "the Word made flesh," the One who also "speaks the words of God."[54] The "apostolic preaching" which is the beginning of tradition, is "expressed in a special way in the inspired books." Renewed understanding of tradition is to be expected, "For there is a growth in the understanding of the realities and the words which have been handed down." There is "a close connection and communication between sacred tradition and Sacred Scripture." Both flow "from the same divine wellspring." Both "are to be accepted and venerated with the same sense of loyalty and reverence." Together they "form one sacred deposit of the word of God, committed to the Church."[55] Including the *Malleus Maleficarum*? Bible readers are instructed to seek out the original intentions of the authors, and have regard to the different literary forms in the Bible, and their historical contexts. It is said to be "common knowledge" that "among all the Scriptures, even those of the New Testament, the Gospels have a special pre-eminence, and rightly so, for they are the principal witness for the life and teaching of the incarnate Word, our savior."[56]

All this accords well with the argument here. But it occasions surprise that the document manages to be pre-critical in some of its teaching, doubtless in order to affirm continuity with previous pronouncements. All 66 books, *plus* those books Protestants call "the Apocrypha" are "written under the inspiration of the Holy Spirit" and "have God as their author." God chooses all the authors, who write down "everything and only those things which He wanted." And the Church, through its Magisterium, manages to get the Bible and tradition just right every time. "But the task of authentically interpreting the word of God, whether written or handed on, has been entrusted exclusively to the living teaching office of the Church, whose authority is exercised in the name of Jesus Christ."[57] For most Protestants the claims made for the teaching office of the Church are **hubris**. While I welcome the unifying of the Bible and tradition as the "one sacred deposit of the word of God," the complacent lack of *any* sense of criticism, or reluctance, or sense that the Church might have got things wrong, sometimes badly wrong, is very disappointing. There is no need for repentance or absolution, for the Church is above making mistakes. It is able to do nothing wrong. And now that easy, undisturbed perfectionism is to be extended to tradition too. Floating serene above the deep ambiguities of Church history, it convinces fewer and fewer people, while its moral indifference alienates more and more potential converts.

All new Christians affirm their continuity with the apostles and the early Church. They acknowledge that Jesus is Lord, the Son of God. They belong to some or other branch of Christ's "Church," which derives its identity from him, and from its relation to other branches of the same tree. This Church, being originally Jewish, accepted the Jewish scriptures, and in order to proclaim its faith that the Messiah had come, produced Gospels which, as *Dei Verbum* insists, "among all the Scriptures ... have a special pre-eminence." The Letters of the New Testament testify to God's coming in Christ and provide much evidence also of how the early churches responded to that unique event. The history of that response did not close at the end of the first century, and remains open today. It is not necessary to draw a firm line between the Bible and tradition. That is why it may be appropriate to think of the Bible, and especially the New Testament, as Primary

Tradition, and the extra-canonical and post-canonical sources as Secondary Tradition. There are several advantages to be gained from approaching it in this way.

First, in a historiographical sense the New Testament, and particularly the Gospels, are literally primary not secondary sources. They are the closest we can get to the events surrounding Jesus. They presuppose the truth of the faith, and the Gospels are written overtly to persuade people who are not Christians to accept the faith as true. They are primary in the historical sense that the apostles knew Jesus, observed him, heard him, and ate and drank with him. The author of one Letter emphasizes the direct experience the apostles had of him – "That which was from the beginning, which we have heard, which we have seen with our eyes, which we have looked upon, and our hands have handled, of the Word of life; (For the life was manifested, and we have seen it, and bear witness...)" (1 John 1:1–3). That intimacy with Jesus makes him primary in the theological sense. We want to know about the divine revelation that was and is him, and that is ultimately more important than secondary details about the organization of the Church or the treatment of heretics. Insofar as these secondary matters can be gleaned from the Bible they will be instructive but not necessarily regulative for ensuing generations.

7 *Let the Spirit show us Jesus*

When a person comes to faith in the Triune God, she or he is likely to see that belief is in some way a gift from God. Understanding faith as a gift does not invalidate the process of intellectual and personal struggle that may have preceded it. The gift of faith then is understood as one that is given by the particular influence of God the Spirit at work among many others. It remains a legitimate question to ask how God, through the Holy Spirit, brings about in the human heart, the human response to God. The answers given will be amazingly varied. Some people will speak of the faith of their parents or their friends, or of the local congregation of Christians. Others will speak of a direct experience of God through a personal or spiritual crisis, or "peak" experience; or of the breaking in of a divine sense of beauty, or of overpowering love. Others may speak of the action of the liturgy, or the hearing of a sermon. There are countless ways by which the gift of faith is given and received.

Since God the Spirit in Christian faith is a Person of God, Christians are licensed to say that the Spirit "speaks" to them, and "speaks" in a way that the Bible, which is not a person, does not and cannot. When God the Spirit summons us to faith, parts of the Bible are likely to have made a decisive impression upon us. This has always been so. Since the Gospels were written expressly to bring people to faith in Jesus Christ, it is hardly surprising that the Spirit should choose to speak through them. This freedom of the Spirit to show us Christ through the Bible (as well as in many other ways) does not require a complex bibliology, an elevation of the Word to a divine or quasi-divine status, in order for us to hear what the Spirit is saying. Indeed, as soon as the Bible begins to "speak" by and for itself, the voice of the Spirit falls silent.

Conclusion

The argument began with the unholy disagreements among Christians and their churches over homosexuality. It was shown in chapter 2 that the confidence of Christians that the Bible "teaches" that homosexual intimacy is wrong, is seriously misplaced. That misplaced confidence gave rise to the question whether the biblical exegesis proscribing homosexual relations was itself evidence for something else, namely, a fear or hatred of homosexual people, or homophobia. A positive answer to that question was postponed, not least because it required that a negative judgment be made about the beliefs, attitudes, and practices of millions of Christians. Now the argument has run its course, we can return to that question.

In one sense the answer is No. Unfortunately Christians are capable of extraordinary prejudice against people they do not understand, except that they are "other." We Christians are living proof of the doctrine that humankind is sinful. There is nothing new in rendering the Bible savage. The argument over homosexuality is the latest episode in a savage "shadow tradition." Homophobia is not required to explain it. But in a second and more important sense the answer is, sadly, Yes. Homophobia is a specific fear, like the fear of black people, women, one's enemies, and so on. The case studies in part II show the proneness of Christians, time after time, to proclaim the Gospel of a loving God while at the same time engaging in denunciations and behaviors that cannot be reconciled with it. And time after time the procedure is similar. Bits of Bible are found which allegedly provide divine guidance in relation to the treatment of all those many minorities the Church suspects. Biblical warrant can invariably be found for atrocious practices. Divine justification is thereby supplied for all manner of cruelties, and the loving Father of all humankind disappears before the punitive god in whose name, and in whose image, a different gospel is proclaimed.

This study may perhaps contribute to the wider problem of biblical interpretation in several ways. First, if its argument is sound it has shown that the theological warfare over homosexuality links the denunciation and intolerance of lesbian and gay people with a tradition of intolerance summed up by the term "savage text." Christians involved in these "discussions" need to know that they are not dealing with a particular "issue" (as Anglican documents suppose), about which a deep division of opinion happens to exist, and which in turn requires to be managed in some procedural way. They are dealing with the latest manifestation of a tradition of savagery. It is necessary to engage with that tradition, theologically and practically. It deserves no place in Christianity at all. There is a better way.

Second, the distress caused to millions of people in our case studies, over centuries, may be seen to underline the Christian horror of idolatry. Yes, idolatry in the Bible and in the Christian tradition is a grave sin. I have contended that when the Bible has become a savage text, it has become an idol, perhaps the most powerful, because the least detected, of all idols. The distress caused to so many people over the centuries as a result of the misuse of the Bible gives weight to the awfulness of idolatry. The idolatry that has been unearthed in these pages is insidious. It is the idolizing of the text in preference to the loving God to whose purposes in Christ the text bears witness. It provides the ultimate excuse for not loving people as the Gospel of Christ commands us.

Third, a different blend of scripture, tradition, and reason is required to do Christian ethics now. The Bible is not enough.

Fourth, urgent action on sexuality is required now. Lesbian and gay people have been turned into a litmus test of conservative and evangelical orthodoxy. Much of the hostility they are currently shown is due to the direct threat they represent to an idolatrous attitude to the Bible. It has little to do even with the visceral response of heterosexual Christians to imagining same-sex intimacy. No, if the just demand for full recognition and inclusion of lesbian and gay people, and their relationships, is met, then cherished views about what the Bible is, and what the Bible allegedly "says," will require modification. They do, of course, require modification. But every savage interpretation of the biblical text has required modification, and this one is no different.

Fifth, people who are attracted to the Person of Christ as the Revealer of God and the clue to the meaning of the universe, should weigh carefully whether the security of their faith has been bought by the exclusion of someone else. The joy of worship, the bondedness of Christian congregations, and the exhilaration of Christian "fellowship" may have a savage side to it. Who is excluded, and why?

Sixth, the wider world needs to know about the savage side to Christianity. When it sacralizes the interests of the American empire, Muslims and other non-Christians rightly discern that the resources of faith are annexed to political and military power.

Seventh, the wider world needs to recognize that fundamentalism in any religion is a human menace. It is founded on spiritual pride, the assurance of certainty, and the certainty that everyone else is wrong.

Eighth, the charge of homophobia regrettably stands. If charity requires a reticence in making it, justice requires the speaking of it. The Christian faith cannot justify violence against anyone. Its founder died a violent death to deal with violence and savagery once and for all.

Glossary

a priori Independent of experience.

aetiological To do with the causes (Greek *aitia*) of something requiring explanation.

Akedah From the Hebrew for "binding" in the story of the binding of Isaac.

allegorically An allegory is a figurative mode of representation which conveys a spiritual or non-literal meaning through a material or literal form.

Anabaptists Christians of the radical Reformation. The name means "rebaptizers." It was used because they did not believe infant baptism was valid, and they rebaptized children when they became capable of profession of faith. Baptists, Mennonites, Plymouth Brethren, and Pentecostalists belong to this tradition.

anagogical From the Greek *anagein*, "to lift up," this refers to things to do with the mystical interpretation of scripture that anticipates the coming Kingdom of God or life after death.

anathema "Set apart," and sometimes banished, excommunicated, or cursed.

Anglican One who is a member of the Church of England: or a church in the Anglican Communion; or a belief or practice of that church or communion. In the United States Anglicans are known as Episcopalians (because they have *episkopoi*, bishops).

Anglican Communion As the British empire spread, the religion of the Church of England followed. Anglican churches were established in many parts of the world. Over 30 autonomous national churches and 12 transnational provinces constitute the present Anglican Communion. See <http://www.anglican.org/church/AngliComm.html>.

anthropocentric Centered on humankind (the Greek *anthrōpos* means "man").

apocalyptic As a noun this refers to a genre of theological writing that developed in sixth-century BCE Judaism. It derives from "apocalypse," also the Greek name for the biblical book, Revelation. Apocalyptic consists of secret meanings about the end of time which are claimed to be "revealed," and are depicted in surreal pictures and terms.

Apocrypha From the Greek term meaning "things having been hidden away," the term is applied to "biblical" books whose authenticity is questioned. In some Protestant Bibles it is the name given to the 15 books which form a full part in the Old Testament of Roman Catholic Bibles. The authenticity and value of these writings was a Reformation issue. Most Protestants are unaware of them.

apostate From the Greek term meaning "standing apart," this was used by Christians of other Christians who were deemed to have renounced their faith.

apostolicity Having derived from an apostle.

Arians Arius (256–336 CE) held that Jesus was fully human but not fully divine. He was afraid that if Jesus was God, Christianity would teach the existence of two Gods, the Father and the Son, so he held that Jesus was created by God, not that he was God.

atonement The process by which God and the world become one ("at-one-ment") through Jesus Christ, by removing what separates them.

Baptists Christians who did not think the Reformation was radical enough. In particular they saw no biblical warrant for the baptism of children, and baptized only adults, by immersion in water (see **Anabaptists**).

biblicism The practice of applying the text of the Bible directly to personal conduct, or to moral, social, or political problems.

bibliolatry Literally the worship of the Bible. The term is used by opponents to draw attention to the elevation of the text of the Bible to divine status. If it is believed that the Bible is free from error, it becomes like God (who alone is to be worshiped) because God is incapable of making mistakes.

black theology A type of liberation theology that seeks to achieve the liberation of black people from oppression.

Body of Christ A metaphor used in the New Testament to refer to the church or churches. It gains its metaphorical impact by suggesting that it presents Christ on earth in the body after his ascension, and by the image of the unity of a single body comprising many limbs and organs.

Calvin, John (1509–64) One of the founders of the Protestant Reformation. There are several branches of the church which derive from Calvin, known as Reformed or Presbyterian (because they have *presbyters* but no bishops). Calvinism is associated with God's absolute sovereignty, and double predestination.

Catechism A book of instruction containing the main doctrines of the Christian faith.

charismatic From the Greek *charisma*, a "gift of grace," which God gives for use in God's service. It is also popularly used of "speaking in tongues" or ecstatic worship which it is assumed God the Holy Spirit inspires.

Christology The study of the Person of Christ.

conservative All Christians are conservative who wish to conserve the teaching of the Bible, or the Bible and tradition, with as little adaptation as possible. Conservative evangelical Christians use the term to define themselves against Protestant liberal, radical, or feminist Christians, against Roman Catholics, and many other Christian groups.

dispensationalism The term derives from the assumption that history in the Bible is arranged in a series of periods or "dispensations."

Docetists From the Greek *dokein*, "to seem," Docetists held that Jesus was divine but that he only *seemed* to have a human body and to have been crucified (see **Gnosticism**).

dogmatic *Dogma* derives from the classical Greek term for "resolution," and means established doctrine. In theology this meaning is distinguished from the popular sense of "opinionated," or "intolerant."

Ebionites The origin of the name is uncertain. Ebionites were Jewish followers of Jesus, who may have derived directly from the earliest (Jewish) Christians. They did not hold the later belief in the preexistence and virgin birth of Christ. They kept the law of the Hebrew scriptures, including male circumcision, and strongly disagreed with Paul's teaching that it was no longer necessary.

enlightened The "Enlightenment" is the name given to the Age of Reason, beginning in the seventeenth century with the philosophy of Descartes; or to an eighteenth-century movement in European and American philosophy which regards reason (and so not religion, revelation, or the Bible) as the basis of knowledge.

episcopate The order of bishops (Greek *episkopoi*) in a church.

Erasmus (c.1466–1536) A Dutch humanist and Roman Catholic theologian, he was also critical of his church. In 1516 he published the New Testament in Greek.

etymological To do with the history or derivation of a word.

evangelical From the Greek *euaggelion*, "gospel." Evangelical Christians encompass a wide range of perspectives: conservative, liberal, reformed, fundamentalist, etc. They hold in common the need for individual sinners to accept Jesus Christ as their savior by an act of faith; and they claim to base their teachings directly on the Bible.

exclusivism In this book, the assumption that some people or groups are excluded from receiving God's grace.

exegesis From the Greek term meaning "to lead out," it is the attempt to draw out meanings from a text, generally using critical methods of interpretation.

Fall The name in Christian theology for the mythological event (Genesis 3) when God banished Eve and Adam from the Garden of Eden for their disobedience.

foreknowledge The ability to know the future. If God knows everything (is "omniscient") then God must know the future. Belief in divine foreknowledge is sometimes linked to the assumption that this knowledge is contained in the Bible.

foreordination A stronger version of divine foreknowledge. God does not merely know the future: God brings it about.

foundational A term borrowed from philosophy to mean to do with the search for rational foundations for certain beliefs which are thought to give these beliefs justificatory support (when none may be available).

fundamentalism This began as a movement in the USA c.1910, stressing the "fundamentals" of Christian faith against liberals, modernists, Roman Catholics, and various sects. The term has come to mean belief in the verbal inerrancy of sacred texts: as such it is also common in the non-Christian religions.

Gnosticism From the Greek *gnōsis*, "knowledge", Gnostics were "people in the know." From the second century CE on they claimed secret knowledge derived from Christian and pagan sources. They sharply distinguished spirit from matter, and held that their souls were fragments of divinity. But they may have been misrepresented by their Catholic opponents, and their Christian beliefs under-emphasized.

Golden Rule The teaching of Jesus about reciprocity: "all things whatsoever ye would that men should do to you, do ye even so to them: for this is the law and the prophets" (Matthew 7:12).

good news The literal meaning of *euaggelion* or "gospel".

Gospel Literally "good news." Mark called his book about Jesus "the gospel" (Mark 1:1). "Gospel" is a literary genre for books about Jesus, some of which were accepted by the early Church as canonical, others not. The term refers to the arrival of the Reign or Kingdom of God, through Jesus Christ.

Great Commandments The commandments of Jesus to love God and to love one's neighbor as oneself (Mark 10:27; Matthew 22:37–40; Luke 10:27; see also John 13:34).

homonym A word the same as another in sound and/or in spelling but different in meaning.

homophobia Literally "fear [*phobia*] of the same [Greek *homos*]." But *homo* is also Latin for "man." In English *homo* is the common prefix of both "homosexual" and "homophobia" and a link between them is commonly (though wrongly) assumed. Homophobia is, then, the fear of people attracted to the same sex, especially men, and the strong disapproval (sometimes leading to violence) of their sexual practices.

Household Codes Principles in the New Testament governing the relations between husbands and wives, parents and children, and masters and slaves. See Colossians 3:18–4:1; Ephesians 5:22–6:9; 1 Peter 2:18–3:7.

hubris Pride.

ideology There are two main sets of uses of this complex term: in the first, it is a system of ideas (religious, philosophical, political); in the second, it is a system of ideas which is thought to misrepresent the interests of the people who hold it, because they have been manipulated in some way into holding false beliefs.

imaginary As a noun, this refers to a belief system of a group which includes myths and/or symbols, some of which may be illusory.

impaired communion The term used by some conservative bishops in the Anglican Communion to express their disapproval of other bishops in the Communion who are associated with the ordination of openly homosexual priests or with the blessing of same-sex unions.

indulgences A major bone of contention at the beginning of the Reformation, an indulgence was the partial remission of the punishment of sin, which was due even after absolution from it. Luther particularly objected to the sale of indulgences.

intuitionism In philosophy this is the view that some knowledge is attainable by a direct mental act or intuition which is capable of bypassing facts or evidence.

J The symbol given to one of the four main sources from which the Pentateuch was compiled (around 850 BCE), so called because of its references to the name of God as Yahweh or Jahweh.

justification by faith The Protestant doctrine that the believer is made right with God solely on the basis of faith in what God has done for him/her through Jesus Christ. "Works," the contribution made by our own attempts to please God, are excluded.

liberalism In theology this may refer to a type of theology which questions traditional thought and the literal interpretation of the Bible, and is open to insights from philosophy and the social sciences. (Latin *liber*, "free"). It is sometimes used to mean the opposite to "conservative."

liberation theologians Theologians belonging to a movement that came to prominence in South America in the 1960s and 1970s. It emphasizes Jesus as the Liberator of the oppressed, and the need for political action to bring about liberation. The Vatican criticizes it for its indebtedness to Marxism.

literalistic Describes a way of reading the Bible which emphasizes the alleged literal meaning of passages, sometimes to the exclusion of all other meanings.

locutionary To do with an act of conveying semantic content in an utterance, considered as independent of the interaction between the speaker and the listener.

Magisterium From the Latin *magister*, "teacher," this is the teaching authority of the Roman Catholic Church, residing in the Pope, the bishops, and their advisors. It believes that, with the help of the Holy Spirit, it always interprets doctrine rightly.

Marcionites Followers of the teaching of Marcion (c.110–60 CE), a bishop who believed that the Christian Gospel was wholly about love, to the exclusion of law. He rejected the Jewish scriptures and their God, and held that Paul alone had fully understood the authentic faith. There were Marcionite churches throughout the Roman empire.

Mennonites A group of Christians who derive from the radical Reformation and the teachings of Menno Simons (1496–1561). They are best known for their dedication to peace and non-violence.

Montanists Followers of Montanus, who preached in the mid-second century. Montanism was an apocalyptic movement which expected a speedy outpouring of the Holy Spirit, which had already descended on Montanus and his two women companions, Prisca and Maximilla, upon the whole Church.

Nag Hammadi Near this village in upper Egypt in 1945, a set of 52 religious and philosophical texts, hidden in an earthenware jar for 1,600 years, was accidentally unearthed, the best known of which is the Gospel of Thomas.

ontological To do with the theory of being (Greek *on*, *ontos*).

Papal Bull From the Latin *bulla*, "seal," a written communication from the Pope.

Parousia From the Greek term meaning "presence with," this refers to the return or Second Coming of Christ.

Pastoral Letters 1 and 2 Timothy, and Titus.

Pentateuch From the Greek for "five" and "case," this is the name for the first five books of the Old Testament (the scrolls were kept in cases).

Pentecostalists Members of a widespread Protestant movement that began in the USA in 1900, and which stresses speaking in tongues, healing, and a literal reading of the Bible.

Plymouth Brethren Established 1827–30, the Brethren came to reject the major Christian denominations, and to found their own movement, based on meeting together only in the name of the Lord Jesus Christ in order to "break bread." The best known Brother is J. N. Darby, whose translation of the Bible is still used. He was the first "dispensationalist" in the modern period.

pogrom Derived from Russian, and meaning a violent attack on a particular group of people, involving the destruction of all their property.

polysemic Having multiple meanings.

positivism Borrowed from philosophy, this term is used loosely here to mean the dogmatic refusal of alternative points of view.

post hoc After the event.

proleptic In theology, to do with the anticipation of the completion of something begun.

Puritans People seeking purity in worship, doctrine, and holiness of life. Puritanism was a movement within Protestant denominations rather than a separate church. Within Anglicanism they held that the Reformation had not gone far enough. "Puritan" was a term of abuse used by their opponents.

Quadrilateral In theology, a series of four sources which, while of possibly unequal weight, combine to form a single method.

Quakers Also known as the Religious Society of Friends, it was founded by George Fox (with others) in seventeenth-century England, and derives from the radical Reformation. The popular name "Quaker" comes from the exhortation of one of them to "tremble [quake] at the word of the Lord." They are best known for their emphases on the "inner light" and on peace and non-violence.

radical Reformation The distinction is commonly made between the "magisterial Reformation" (Lutheran and Reformed) and the "radical Reformation," which was more radical in its teachings. These included believers' baptism, the common ownership of property, and pacifism. Anabaptists were the biggest group.

rationalization In social theory, the provision of inadequate reasons or excuses for something instead of an explanation for it.

redactor An author who puts together a text from different sources. "Redaction criticism" is the attempt by scholars to discover what the author intended in creating the work.

Reformed Either the churches established at the Reformation, or particular churches (Presbyterian or Calvinist) which base themselves on the teaching of John Calvin.

retributivism In ethics, law, and theology, the belief that justice is served by retribution, understood as the infliction of punishment somehow equivalent to the seriousness of a crime, regardless of its benefits or the likelihood of remedial consequences.

rule of faith "Rule" (Latin *regula*, Greek *kanōn*) means a standard by which something can be tested, serving as its norm or measure. The earliest rule of faith was reported by Irenaeus in the second century. It functioned as an early creed.

sanctification The process of becoming holy (from the Latin *sanctus*, "holy").

Scripture Principle The Protestant principle that matters of faith and practice must be established on the basis of scripture alone (*sola scriptura*), when read primarily in its plain or straightforward sense.

Seven Deadly Sins A list of sins used by the medieval Church in its moral teachings: lust, gluttony, avarice, laziness, anger, envy, and pride. They are not classified together in the Bible or referred to collectively among Protestants.

substitutionary In theology, the extraordinary belief, held by evangelical and fundamentalist Christians, that God punished Jesus on the Cross, instead of punishing us, for our sins. Christ becomes our substitute.

supercessionism The belief that the New Covenant established between God and humanity in Jesus Christ supersedes the covenant in the Old Testament given to the Jews.

texts of terror The title of a work by the feminist theologian Phyllis Trible in 1984, this refers to biblical stories containing violence against women, and is now more widely used.

Torah In Hebrew this means "law," "teaching," or "instruction," "scribe." It refers to the Law of Moses, or to the Pentateuch.

triune Literally "three in one," so to do with God as Trinity.

Unitarians Associated with Socinus (1539–1604), Unitarians belonged to the radical Reformation. They held that the unity of God could not be reconciled with the traditional doctrine of the Trinity. They believe in the humanity of Jesus and that the one God raised him from the dead. Unitarians today are known for their liberal theology and universal outlook.

universalism The belief that all people will ultimately obtain salvation.

Vulgate An early fifth-century Latin translation of Hebrew and Greek editions of the biblical books undertaken largely by Jerome (around 340–420 CE).

works The term is part of the controversy since the Reformation on the place, if any, of one's own efforts (works) in attaining salvation, which is principally an unmerited gift of grace.

Notes

Chapter 1   The "Savage Text"?

1   All Bible quotations in this chapter are from the New International Version.

2   Maggi Dawn, "Whose Text Is It Anyway? Limit and Freedom in Interpretation," in Duncan Dormor and Jeremy Morris (eds.), *An Acceptable Sacrifice? Homosexuality and the Church* (London: SPCK, 2007), 10–21: 14.

3   For example by Malise Ruthven, *Fundamentalism: The Search for Meaning* (Oxford: Oxford University Press, 2004), and several earlier works of James Barr.

4   London: SPCK, 1978.

5   London: SPCK, 1963.

6   London: SPCK, 1988.

7   London: SPCK, 2004.

8   These beliefs are held by the British Modern Churchpeople's Union, a group of Christians who rejoice in "liberal theology," and of which I am a member.

9   *The American Heritage® Dictionary of the English Language*, 4th edn. (Boston: Houghton Mifflin, 2004). June 25 2007. <http://dictionary.reference.com/browse/type>.

10   Karl Barth, *Church Dogmatics*, I.2 (Edinburgh: T&T Clark, 1963), 457 (emphasis added). Readers of Barth will know that this statement is heavily qualified later.

11   Ibid. 480.

Chapter 2 "Vile Affections": The Bible and Homosexuality

1 New International Version.
2 New American Standard Bible.
3 Congregation for the Doctrine of the Faith, *Letter to the Catholic Bishops on the Pastoral Care of Homosexual Persons* (1986), section 3. <http://www.vatican.va/roman_curia/congregations/cfaith/documents/rc_con_cfaith_doc_19861001_homosexual-persons_en.html>. The letter was issued by Cardinal Joseph Ratzinger, now Pope Benedict XVI.
4 Gareth Moore, OP, *A Question of Truth: Christianity and Homosexuality* (New York: Continuum, 2003) 93. The references where the term is used to mean "passions" (not "suffering") are 1 Thessalonians 4:5, Galatians 5:24, Romans 7:5, Colossians 3:5.
5 Dale Martin, *Sex and the Single Saviour* (Louisville, KY: Westminster John Knox Press, 2006), 65–76.
6 Moore, *A Question of Truth*, 91.
7 See the argument of Eugene F. Rogers, Jr., *Sexuality and the Christian Body* (Oxford: Blackwell, 1999), 64–6.
8 See the argument of James E. Miller, "The Practices of Romans 1:26: Homosexual or Heterosexual?", *Novum Testamentum*, 37 (1995), 1, and cited in Moore, *A Question of Truth*, 98.
9 Moore, *A Question of Truth*, 89.
10 Robin Scroggs, *The New Testament and Homosexuality* (Philadelphia: Fortress Press, 1983). And see Moore, *A Question of Truth*, 94.
11 A point made in 1989 by the Anglican bishop Peter Coleman in his *Gay Christians: A Moral Dilemma* (London: SCM Press, 1989), 88.
12 Martin, *Sex and the Single Saviour*, 55.
13 Emphasis added.
14 House of Bishops' Group on Issues in Human Sexuality, *Some Issues in Human Sexuality: A Guide to the Debate* (London: Church House Publishing, 2003), 4.3.26 (p. 137).
15 Ibid. 4.3.53 (p. 143).
16 Martin, *Sex and the Single Saviour*, 41.
17 Moore, *A Question of Truth*, 110.
18 Martin, *Sex and the Single Saviour*, 61.

19 Congregation for the Doctrine of the Faith, *Letter to the Catholic Bishops*, section 6.

20 Diarmaid MacCulloch, *Reformation: Europe's House Divided 1490–1700* (London: Penguin Books, 2004), 623.

21 Almost no "sisters in Christ" mount such daft arguments.

22 At the time of finishing this book (August 2007) cancellation of the conference was being openly discussed, due to the bickering among bishops about who was being invited.

23 Lambeth Conference 1998, Resolution 1.10c. See <http://www.lambethconference.org/resolutions/1998/1998–1–10.cfm>.

24 Emphasis added.

25 The Church of England case for this is set out in *Marriage in Church after Divorce* (London: Church House Publishing, 2000). I agree with it, but not with the inconsistency of my church in deploying a tortuous scriptural revisionism in order to reach its conclusions on remarriage while retaining its ostrich-like obstinacy over the recognition of same-sex unions.

26 Resolution 1.10d (emphasis added).

27 For a detailed criticism of this document, see Adrian Thatcher, "Some Issues with 'Some Issues in Human Sexuality,'" *Theology and Sexuality*, 11/3 (May 2005), 9–30.

28 House of Bishops' Group, *Some Issues in Human Sexuality*, 2.1 (pp. 37–9).

29 Ibid. 2.1.1 (p. 37).

30 Ibid. 2.1.2 (p. 37).

31 Ibid. 2.1.7 (p. 38; emphases added).

32 Ibid. 2.5–2.6 (pp. 52–8).

33 *Catechism of the Catholic Church* (London: Geoffrey Chapman, 1994), para. 2357 (pp. 504–5; emphasis added).

34 Southern Baptist Convention Position Statement: "Sexuality." See <http://www.sbc.net/aboutus/pssexuality.asp>.

35 Southern Baptist Convention Basic Beliefs: "The Scriptures." <http://www.sbc.net/aboutus/basicbeliefs.asp>.

36 House of Bishops' Group, *Some Issues in Human Sexuality*, 3.4.8, 3.4.20, 3.4.23 (pp. 79–80, 82).

37 Ibid. 3.4.49, 3.4.50 (pp. 89–90).

38 For different and further damaging criticisms of the bishops' use of this text, see Andrew Mein, "Threat and Promise: The Old Testament on Sexuality," in Dormor and Morris, *An Acceptable Sacrifice?*, 22–32: 26–9.

39 See Michael Northcott, *An Angel Directs the Storm: Apocalyptic Religion & American Empire* (London: I. B. Tauris, 2004), 48.

40 House of Bishops' Group, *Some Issues in Human Sexuality*, 3.4.56 (p. 91).

41 For this point, and the reduction of complementarity to theological rubble, see Moore, *A Question of Truth*, 127–34, and throughout.

42 Mark D. Jordan, *The Ethics of Sex* (Oxford: Blackwell, 2002), 151.

43 Theodore W. Jennings, Jr., *The Man Jesus Loved: Homoerotic Narratives from the New Testament* (Cleveland, OH: Pilgrim Press, 2003), 22.

44 Ibid. 113.

45 Ibid. 131–40.

46 Theodore W. Jennings, Jr., *Jacob's Wound: Homoerotic Narrative in the Literature of Ancient Israel* (New York: Continuum, 2005), 3–80.

47 Congregation for Catholic Education, *Instruction Concerning the Criteria for the Discernment of Vocations with regard to Persons with Homosexual Tendencies in view of their Admission to the Seminary and to Holy Orders* (2005). <http://www.vatican.va/roman_curia/congregations/ccatheduc/documents/rc_con_ccatheduc_doc_20051104_istruzione_en.html>.

48 Jennings, *Jacob's Wound*, 227.

49 Martin, *Sex and the Single Saviour*, 50.

Chapter 3   "Cursed Be Canaan!": The Bible, Racism, and Slavery

1 Gerhard von Rad, *Genesis* (London: SCM Press, 1961), 131–2.

2 See John Rogerson, *Genesis 1–11* (Sheffield: Sheffield Academic Press, 1991), 72–3.

3 David M. Goldenberg, *The Curse of Ham: Race and Slavery in Early Judaism, Christianity, and Islam* (Princeton, NJ: Princeton University Press, 2003), 175 (author's emphasis).

4 Alexander Crummell, "The Negro Race Not under a Curse: An Examination of Genesis IX. 25," in id., *The Future of Africa, being Addresses, Sermons, etc., etc., Delivered in the Republic of Liberia* (New York, 1862), 327–8: cited in Goldenberg, *The Curse of Ham*, 176.

5 Goldenberg, *The Curse of Ham*, 178.

6 Kelly Brown Douglas, *What's Faith Go To Do with It? Black Bodies/Christian Souls* (Maryknoll, NY: Orbis Books, 2005), 129–31.

7   Ibid. 3–4.

8   Ibid. 5.

9   *Oxford English Dictionary*, 2nd edn. (1989). See <http://dictionary.oed. com/cgi/entry/50195905>.

10 Goldenberg, *The Curse of Ham*, 13.

11 On a different interpretation, Aaron's and Miriam's crime *is* racism, which the biblical writer abhors. "He obviously thinks of it as evil and totally against the will and designs of God. So the racists in the story are punished. The author cleverly adds an ironic twist: those who reject Moses' black wife are made 'white as snow'; that is, they become lepers, the worst type of punishment there is." See John Holder, "The Issue of Race: A Search for a Biblical/Theological Perspective," *Journal of Religious Thought*, 49/2 (Winter 1992/Spring 1993), 44–59: 50.

12 "Ethiopian" is used interchangeably with "Kushite" in the Authorized Version. In Numbers 12:1, the AV uses "Kushite" as the marginal alternative to "Ethiopian."

13 Goldenberg, *The Curse of Ham*, 23.

14 Cain Hope Felder, "Afrocentrism, the Bible, and the Politics of Difference," *Journal of Religious Thought*, 50/1–2 (Fall 1993/Spring 1994), 45–57: 47.

15 Goldenberg, *The Curse of Ham*, 141–56.

16 Ibid. 47–8.

17 Augustine, *Commentary on the Psalms*, 71.12. See Goldenberg, *The Curse of Ham*, 22.

18 Goldenberg, *The Curse of Ham*, 49.

19 Ibid. 142.

20 Wayne A. Meeks, "The 'Haustafeln' and American Slavery: A Hermeneutical Challenge," in Eugene H. Lovering, Jr. and Jerry L. Sumney (eds.), *Theology and Ethics in Paul and his Interpreters* (Nashville: Abingdon Press, 1996), 232–53: 232.

21 Willard M. Swartley, *Slavery, Sabbath, War & Women* (Scottdale, PA: Herald Press, 1983). I apologize to women readers if they should think their sex is an "issue," while the sex of men is not, in this book.

22 John Henry Hopkins, *A Scriptural, Ecclesiastical, and Historical View of Slavery, from the Days of the Patriarch Abraham, to the Nineteenth Century* (New York: Pooley & Co., 1864), 16–17, cited in Swartley, *Slavery*, 31.

23 Swartley, *Slavery*, 33.

24 Ibid. 34–7.
25 Ibid. 39–44.
26 Ibid. 53.
27 Ibid. 53–4.
28 Diana Hayes, "Reflections on Slavery," in Charles E. Curran (ed.), *Change in Official Catholic Moral Teachings* (New York and Mahwah, NJ: Paulist Press, 2003), 65–75: 65.
29 Swartley, *Slavery*, 61.
30 Renita J. Weems, "Reading *Her Way* through the Struggle: African American Women and the Bible," in Cain Hope Felder (ed.), *Stony the Road We Trod: African American Biblical Interpretation* (Minneapolis: Fortress Press, 1991), 57–80: 60.
31 Ibid. 61.
32 Ibid. 64.
33 Douglas, *What's Faith Got to Do with It?*, 164.
34 Weems, "Reading *Her Way* through the Struggle," 65.
35 Vincent L. Wimbush, "The Bible and African Americans: An Outline of an Interpretative History," in Felder (ed.), *Stony the Road We Trod*, 81–97: 86.
36 Weems, "Reading *Her Way* through the Struggle," 66.
37 James H. Cone, "Theology's Great Sin: Silence in the Face of White Supremacy," *Black Theology: An International Journal*, 2/2 (July 2004), 139–52: 142.
38 This point is trenchantly argued by Rodney Stark, *For the Glory of God: How Monotheism Led to Reformations, Science, Witch-Hunts, and the End of Slavery* (Princeton: Princeton University Press, 2003), 291–366.

Chapter 4   "The Great Day of Wrath": The Bible and the End

1 See Alister E. McGrath, *Science & Religion: An Introduction* (Oxford: Blackwell, 1999), 11.
2 There will be more on the "plain sense" in part III.
3 See Tim Gorringe, "Political Readings of Scripture," in John Barton (ed.), *The Cambridge Companion to Biblical Interpretation* (Cambridge: Cambridge University Press, 1998), 67–80: 68.
4 Mark 13:1–37; Matthew 24–5; Luke 20:20–37.

5   1 Thessalonians 4:13–5:11; parts of 1 Corinthians 15:12–58.

6   "Prevent" in Elizabethan English means "precede," "go before."

7   It is possible Paul knew the saying of Jesus preserved in Matthew 16:27 ("For the Son of man shall come in the glory of his Father with his angels …").

8   He says something similar in 1 Corinthians 15:51 – "Behold, I shew you a mystery; We shall not all sleep, but we shall all be changed."

9   The "Left Behind" series of seven books by Tim LaHaye and Jerry Jenkins has sold more than 50 million copies.

10 <http://www.leftbehind.com>, accessed Feb. 28, 2007.

11 And see Mark 13:14–27.

12 The meaning of these seals was central to the Branch Davidian sect which was raided by the American government in Waco, Texas, in 1993, leading to the loss of 80 members of the sect, including 20 children.

13 Northcott, *An Angel Directs the Storm*, 15 (author's emphases).

14 Ibid. 44.

15 P. Boyer, *When Time Shall Be No More: Prophecy Belief in Modern American Culture* (Cambridge, MA: Belknap, 1992), 141. For further references see Crawford Gribben, "Rapture Fictions and the Changing Evangelical Condition", *Literature and Theology*, 18/1 (Mar. 2004), 77–94. For more examples see the references in this article.

16 See Jim Wallis, *God's Politics: Why the Right Gets It Wrong and the Left Doesn't Get It* (Oxford: Lion Publishing, 2006), and Randall Balmer, *Thy Kingdom Come: How the Religious Right Distorts the Faith and Threatens America (an Evangelical's Lament)* (New York: Basic Books, 2007).

17 See MacCulloch, *Reformation*, 527.

18 Northcott, *An Angel Directs the Storm*, 88.

19 Ibid. 66.

20 Ibid. 89.

21 Ibid. 75.

22 Ibid. 105.

23 Judith Kovacs and Christopher Rowland, *Revelation* (Oxford: Blackwell, 2004), 21.

24 Josephus, *War of the Jews* VI.9.3. <http://www.sacred-texts.com/jud/josephus/index.htm>.

25 *Catechism of the Catholic Church*, paras. 675–6 (p. 155).

26 Kovacs and Rowland, *Revelation*, 248.

Chapter 5 "Take Now Thy Son": The Bible and Children

1 For an exhaustive treatment of the subject, see Marcia J. Bunge (ed.), *The Child in Christian Thought* (Grand Rapids, MI: Eerdmans, 2001).

2 See Stephen Lake, *Let the Children Come to Communion* (London: SPCK, 2006).

3 See Judith M. Gundry-Wolf, "The Least and the Greatest: Children in the New Testament," in Marcia J. Bunge (ed.), *The Child in Christian Thought* (Grand Rapids, MI: Eerdmans, 2001), 29–60: 38.

4 Herbert Anderson and Susan B.W. Johnson, *Regarding Children: A New Respect for Childhood and Families* (Louisville, KY: Westminster John Knox Press, 1995), 10.

5 See ibid. 20–1.

6 Some references to children in the Gospels are probably intended to apply to adults, in their childlike faith or in their relation to the heavenly Father. On this see Adrian Thatcher, *Theology and Families* (Oxford: Blackwell), 30.

7 Hugh Pyper, "Children," in Adrian Hastings, Alistair Mason, and Hugh Pyper (eds.), *The Oxford Companion to Christian Thought* (Oxford: Oxford University Press, 2000), 110.

8 For more of the same see Proverbs 29:15; Ecclesiasticus 30:1–13.

9 The Authorized Version is almost unintelligible here, so I have used the Revised English Bible.

10 John Shelby Spong, *The Sins of Scripture* (New York: HarperSanFrancisco, 2005), 146.

11 High on the list of indictable works is Søren Kierkegaard's *Fear and Trembling* (1843) (Oxford: Oxford University Press, 1939; Harmondsworth: Penguin Books, 2005).

12 Kierkegaard, *Fear and Trembling* (1939 edn.), 39.

13 Ibid. 43, and throughout.

14 Jon D. Levenson, *The Death and Resurrection of the Beloved Son: The Transformation of Child Sacrifice in Judaism and Christianity* (New Haven: Yale University Press, 1993), 3–4.

15 Ibid. 36 (author's emphasis).

16 Ibid. 15.

17 New International Version. The AV is opaque.

18 See Francesca Stavrakopoulou, "Child Sacrifice in the Ancient World: Blessings for the Beloved," in L. Brockliss and G. Rousseau (eds.), *Childhood, Violence and the Western Tradition* (Oxford: Oxford University Press, forthcoming).

19 Ibid.

20 Carol Delaney, *Abraham on Trial: The Social Legacy of Biblical Myth* (Princeton: Princeton University Press, 1998).

21 Francesca Stavrakopolou, *King Manasseh and Child Sacrifice: Biblical Distortions of Historical Realities* (Berlin: Walter de Gruyter, 2004), 318, 319–20.

22 David Ford, *Christian Wisdom: Desiring God and Learning in Love* (Cambridge: Cambridge University Press, 2007), 231 (author's emphasis).

23 Delaney, *Abraham on Trial*, 6.

24 Levenson, *The Death and Resurrection of the Beloved Son*, 111.

25 Delaney, *Abraham on Trial*, 101.

26 Richard Holloway, *Godless Morality* (Edinburgh: Canongate, 1999), 6–7.

27 See "Letter 1: Sarah to Abraham," in Philip R. Davies (ed.), *Yours Faithfully: Virtual Letters from the Bible* (London: Equinox, 2004), 1–3, for an imaginative first-person account of her incredulity and anger.

28 See "Letter 2: Isaac to Abraham," ibid. 5–22.

29 Delaney thinks ancient paternity also creates the power to destroy life. See *Abraham on Trial*, 7, 109.

30 Stavrakopolou, *King Manasseh and Child Sacrifice*, 321.

31 Christian theology has several alternatives. One is to recognize the inevitability of the death of Jesus being understood in terms of the Jewish sacrificial system. Another is to read the crucifixion of Jesus as the total giving of his life, to the Father and to us, in an act of divine love. Another, following the argument of the letter to the Hebrews, is to see the crucifixion as the sacrifice that renders the whole wretched system of sacrifice unnecessary and redundant. Another is to stress the centrality of the doctrine of the incarnation in showing how God and humankind become one.

32 Delaney, *Abraham on Trial*, 233; ch. 10 is entitled "Sacrificing our Children."

33 Northcott, *An Angel Directs the Storm*, ch. 3, "The Unveiling of Empire."

34 Ibid. 97. He acknowledges his debt here to the thesis of Carolyn Marvin and David W. Ingle in *Blood Sacrifice and the Nation: Totem Rituals and the American Flag* (Cambridge: Cambridge University Press, 1999).

35 Northcott, *An Angel Directs the Storm*, 98.

36 Wilfred Owen's poem of that name ("It is sweet and right to die for your country") is the best-known poem of World War I. The title is a maxim of Horace that Owen in the poem calls "the old Lie."

37 Delaney, *Abraham on Trial*, 234 (author's emphasis).

38 Ibid., ch. 2.

39 Gill Cooke, "Christian Forgiveness in Rampton Special Hospital," *Higher Calling* (University of Liverpool Chaplaincy Newsletter), 3.

40 Delaney, *Abraham on Trial*, 235–6.

41 Marilyn McCord Adams, *Christ and Horrors: The Coherence of Christology* (Cambridge: Cambridge University Press, 2006), 9 (author's emphasis). Adams has in her sights sociological objections to traditional Christology, but the principle remains the same here.

42 Delaney, *Abraham on Trial*, 250.

43 I develop this contrast further in my "Beginning Again with Jesus," in Annemie Dillen and Didier Pollefeyt (eds.), *Children's Voices: Children's Perspectives in Ethics, Theology, and Religious Education* (Leuven: Peeters, forthcoming).

Chapter 6 "Thou Shalt Not Suffer a Witch to Live": The Bible, Jews, and Women

1 Gerd Lüdemann, *The Unholy in Holy Scripture: The Dark Side of the Bible*, tr. John Bowden (London: SCM Press, 1997), 87.

2 Ibid. 89.

3 Ibid. 91.

4 For example, 2 Samuel 1:16; 1 Kings 2:37; Jeremiah 26:15, 51:35.

5 Lüdemann, *The Unholy in Holy Scripture*, 93.

6 Acts 2:22–3, 2:36, 3:13–15, 7:52.

7 Eusebius, *Church History*, 3.5.2–7. Christian Classics Ethereal Library. <http://www.ccel.org/ccel/schaff/npnf201.iii.viii.v.html>.

8 See, for example, its hosting by the Humanitas International website, <http://www.humanitas-international.org/showcase/chronography/documents/luther-jews.htm>.

9 Luther, *On the Jews and their Lies* (1543), pt. 11; at the Humanitas International website (see n. 8 above).

10 John 9:22; 34, 12:42, 16:2.

11 For the arguments leading to these conclusions, see Ulrich Luz, *The Theology of the Gospel of Matthew* (Cambridge: Cambridge University Press, 1995), 11–21.

12 MacCulloch, *Reformation*, 572, 563.

13 P. G. Maxwell-Stuart, *An Abundance of Witches: The Great Scottish Witch-Hunt* (Stroud: Tempus Publishing, 2005), 150.

14 Heinrich Kramer and James Sprenger, *Malleus Maleficarum* (1948 edn.), tr. Montague Summers (Kessinger Publishing, n.p., n.d.), 1.1 (p. 3). Leviticus 19:31, 20:6, and Deuteronomy 18:10–11 are all cited as further evidence.

15 The following quotations from *Malleus Maleficarum* are from this section, pp. 41–7 in Kramer and Sprenger. This work precedes the Authorized Version of the Bible. These writers of course worked with the Vulgate, and when I cite their use of scripture, I use Kramer and Sprenger's text. Use, not accuracy, is the issue here.

16 The Authorized Version (oddly) has "enemy" here. The **Vulgate** has "woman" (*mulieris*), which I follow here.

17 By our standards, these are not the most offensive verses in this chapter. Note particularly the permission to divorce a wife "if she go not as thou wouldest have her …" (25:26).

18 This material is introduced by the apparatus of neutrality ("Others again have propounded other reasons …"). It is clear the authors accept these reasons, and weave them into their cumulative case.

19 For a full description of what constituted witchcraft, and how the Church of Scotland dealt with it, see Maxwell-Stuart, *An Abundance of Witches*.

20 James Dalrymple, *Institutions of the Laws of Scotland* (1681), bk. 1, title 3, cited in Maxwell-Stuart, *An Abundance of Witches*, 74.

21 See, most recently, Walter Kasper, "Anti-Semitism: A Wound to be Healed," (2003) and the references there. <http://www.vatican.va/roman_curia/pontifical_councils/chrstuni/relations-jews-docs/rc_pc_chrstuni_doc_20030908_kasper-antisemitismo_en.html>.

22 The exact number of deaths has been sharply contested, and exaggerated. I follow the cautious comment of MacCulloch (*Reformation*, 563): "There is now general agreement among historians that between 1400 and 1800, between forty and fifty thousand people died in Europe and colonial north America on charges of witchcraft."

23   MacCulloch, *Reformation*, 701.
24   The phrase belongs to T. Richard Snyder, *The Protestant Ethic and the Spirit of Punishment* (Grand Rapids, MI: Eerdmans, 2001).
25   See ibid. for the arguments.
26   See the excellent work of Nancy Eiesland on this topic, for example, *The Disabled God: Towards a Liberation Theology of Disability* (Nashville, TN: Abingdon Press, 1994).

Chapter 7   Faith in the Book or Faith in God?

1   Martin Luther, *Preface to the Epistles of St. James and St. Jude* (1522), cited in Barth, *Church Dogmatics*, I.2 (p. 478).
2   The Reformers notoriously disagreed among themselves about what happened in the Eucharist.
3   MacCulloch, *Reformation*, 131 (emphasis added).
4   Ibid.
5   These included the Latin translation of the Greek *mustērion* as *sacramentum* or sacrament in Ephesians 5:31–2: the Latin rendition of "Repent" in Matthew 4:17 as "Do penance": the Latin rendition of the angel's words to Mary as "full of grace," when the Greek allowed only "one who has found favor"; and the omission of half of a proof text for the Trinity at 1 John 5:7–8 since it was not in the Greek manuscripts Erasmus used (nor in most others either).
6   Council of Trent (1546), session 4, "Decree concerning the Canonical Scriptures," tr. J. Waterworth (London: Dolman, 1848). <http://history.hanover.edu/texts/trent/ct04.html>.
7   Article 6 of the 39 Articles of Religion.
8   Barth, *Church Dogmatics*, I.2 (p. 476).
9   Council of Trent (1546), session 4 (emphasis added).
10   Barth, *Church Dogmatics*, I.2 (p. 478).
11   See e.g. Alister E. McGrath, *The Christian Theology Reader*, 2nd edn. (Oxford: Blackwell, 2001), 94–5.
12   Peter Harrison, *The Bible, Protestantism, and the Rise of Natural Science* (Cambridge: Cambridge University Press, 1998), 4.
13   Ibid. 4.
14   Ibid. 8.

15 Francis Bacon, *The Advancement of Learning*, bk. I, ed. W. A. Armstrong (London: Athlone Press, 1975), i.3 (p. 55). In this passage the two books are called "the book of God's word" and "the book of God's works."

16 David S. Katz, *God's Last Words: Reading the English Bible from the Reformation to Fundamentalism* (New Haven: Yale University Press, 2004), 97.

17 Harrison, *The Bible*, 83.

18 MacCulloch, *Reformation*, 631. See also Harrison, *The Bible*, 85.

19 Katz, *God's Last Words*, 38, 44.

20 Thomas Hobbes, *Behemoth*, ed. F. Tönnies (London, 1889), 21–2, cited in Katz, *God's Last Words*, 41.

21 Katz, *God's Last Words*, 52 (emphasis added).

22 Scripture, tradition, and reason are thought to be the sources of theology. John Wesley added experience (the so-called Wesleyan **Quadrilateral**).

23 MacCulloch, *Reformation*, 149.

24 Ibid. 167.

25 Ezekiel 44:2 and Isaiah 7:14. See MacCulloch, *Reformation*, 101, 613.

26 MacCulloch, *Reformation*, 379.

27 Article 6 of the 39 Articles of Religion.

28 Richard Hooker, *Ecclesiastical Polity, Books I–IV*, ed. E. Rhys, vol. 1 (London: J. M. Dent, 1907; repr. Everyman's Library, 1925), 1.14.1 (p. 215).

29 Ibid. 1.14.2 (p. 216).

30 Ibid. 1.14.3 (p. 217; emphasis added).

31 Ibid. 1.14 (pp. 236–7).

32 Ibid. 1.14 (p. 242).

33 There is a full and fair account of the principle of indifference or *adiaphora* and the difficulty of applying it, in *The Lambeth Commission on Communion* [The Windsor Report] (London: Church House Publishing, 2004), sections 87–96. Online at <http://www.anglicancommunion.org/windsor2004/downloads/windsor2004full.pdf>.

34 Hooker, *Ecclesiastical Polity*, 1.14.6 (p. 273).

35 Bart D. Ehrman, *Misquoting Jesus: The Story Behind who Changed the Bible and Why* (New York: HarperSanFrancisco, 2005), 83–4 (emphasis added).

36 Bart D. Ehrman, *Lost Christianities: The Battles for Scripture and the Faiths We Never Knew* (New York: Oxford University Press, 2003), 219.

37 Ibid. 217.

38 Ibid. 221–7. And see Ehrman, *Misquoting Jesus*, 151–76.

39 Ehrman, *Lost Christianities*, 59.

40 John Henson, *Good as New: A Radical Retelling of the Scriptures* (New York: O Books, 2004), 63–81 (where it is entitled "Thought-Provoking Sayings").

41 Ehrman, *Lost Christianities*, 231.

42 Richard J. Bauckham, "Jude," in Bruce M. Metzger and Michael D. Coogan (eds.), *The Oxford Companion to the Bible* (New York: Oxford University Press, 1993), 395–7: 396.

43 Jennifer Wright Knust, *Abandoned to Lust: Sexual Slander and Ancient Christianity* (New York: Columbia University Press, 2006), 49.

44 Ibid. 3.

45 *Dogmatic Constitution on Divine Revelation: Dei Verbum* (1965), sections 9–10. Online at <http://www.vatican.va/archive/hist_councils/ii_vatican_council/documents/vat-ii_const_19651118_dei-verbum_en.html>.

46 Ehrman, *Lost Christianities*, 257.

47 The content of Ehrman's *Lost Christianities*.

48 Adrian Thatcher, *Truly a Person, Truly God* (London: SPCK, 1990).

49 MacCulloch, *Reformation*, 160.

50 Ibid. 245.

51 Ibid. 275.

52 Ibid. 485.

53 Ibid. 676.

54 See David Martin, *Does Christianity Cause War?* (Oxford: Oxford University Press, 1997).

55 Translated by Bart D. Ehrman, in Ehrman, *Lost Scriptures*, 30.

Chapter 8   On Not Being a "People of the Book"

1 "Scriptural reasoning," emanating from Cambridge, UK, is a good example of this new genre. See the Society for Scriptural Reasoning [SR] website, <http://etext.lib.virginia.edu/journals/jsrforum/>. David Ford and C. C. Pecknold (eds.), *The Promise of Scriptural Reasoning* (Oxford: Blackwell, 2006), contains 14 distinguished essays, but the

paucity of references throughout to Jesus Christ may indicate both the further erosion of Christocentric biblical interpretation and the spread of "bookishness" into Christian theology.

2   John Barton, *People of the Book? The Authority of the Bible in Christianity*, rev. edn. (London: SPCK, 1993), 1.

3   Emphasis added. And see Matthew 17:5, Luke 9:35.

4   Cambridge: Cambridge University Press, 2003.

5   John Webster, *Holy Scripture: A Dogmatic Sketch* (Cambridge: Cambridge University Press, 2003), 31, 2.

6   Ibid. 3, citing approvingly G. Dehn, *Man and Revelation* (London: Hodder & Stoughton, 1936), 8.

7   Webster, *Holy Scripture*, 23, 9.

8   Ibid. 24.

9   Ibid. 27.

10   Ibid. 25. The term is borrowed from G. C. Berkouwer.

11   Ibid. 70.

12   Ibid. 78.

13   Ibid. 46, 51 (author's emphasis).

14   Ibid. 44, 53, 57, 60, 62, 63.

15   Ibid. 82, 69, 87, 102 (author's emphasis).

16   New International Version.

17   Ellen F. Davis and Richard B. Hays (eds.), Introduction to *The Art of Reading Scripture* (Grand Rapids, MI: Eerdmans, 2003), 16 (emphasis added).

18   William Stacy Johnson, "Reading the Scriptures Faithfully in a Postmodern Age," in Davis and Hays (eds.), *The Art of Reading Scripture*, 109–24: 109.

19   Walter Brueggemann, "Biblical Authority in the Postcritical Period," in id., *The Book That Breathes New Life: Scriptural Authority and Biblical Theology* (Minneapolis: Fortress Press, 2005), 3–19, 20.

20   Martin, *Sex and the Single Saviour*, 1.

21   Ibid. 5, 2.

22   Brueggemann, *The Book That Breathes New Life*, 6 (author's emphasis). See also, pp. 14, 16.

23   Ibid. 16.

24   Ford, *Christian Wisdom*, 58.

25   Ibid. 19.

26 Ibid. 20 (author's emphasis).

27 Ludwig Wittgenstein, *Philosophical Investigations*, tr. G. E. M. Anscombe (Oxford: Blackwell, 1972), section 123 (p. 49).

28 See Gavin d'Costa, "Revelation, Scripture and Tradition: Some Comments on John Webster's Conception of 'Holy Scripture'," *International Journal of Systematic Theology*, 6/4 (Oct. 2004), 337–50: "the drift of his [Webster's] position actually erodes his goal, for scripture's objectivity and authority is only safeguarded by an interpretative tradition that must *share* in the *authority* of scripture to secure scripture's authority" (p. 342; author's emphases).

29 Christopher Evans, *Is "Holy Scripture" Christian? And Other Questions* (London: SCM Press, 1971), 17.

30 See Thatcher, *Theology and Families*, ch. 2; id., *Marriage after Modernity: Christian Marriage in Postmodern Times* (Sheffield and New York: Sheffield Academic Press/New York University Press, 1999), 12–25: Elizabeth Stuart and Adrian Thatcher, *People of Passion: What the Churches Teach about Sex* (London: Mowbray, 1997), ch. 10; Thatcher, *Liberating Sex: A Christian Sexual Theology* (London: SPCK, 1993), ch. 2.

31 See Katz, *God's Last Words*, 112, and the sources cited on p. 336.

32 Charles H. Cosgrove, *Appealing to Scripture in Moral Debate: Five Hermeneutical Rules* (Grand Rapids, MI: Eerdmans, 2002), 2 (author's emphasis).

33 Davis and Hays (eds.), *The Art of Reading Scripture*, 1–5.

34 Keith Ward, *What the Bible Really Teaches: A Challenge for Fundamentalists* (London: SPCK, 2004), ch. 2.

35 Ibid. 27.

36 Weems, "Reading *Her Way* through the Struggle," 64 (author's emphasis). See chapter 3 above.

37 Ibid. 65.

38 Barth, *Church Dogmatics*, I.2 (p. 478).

39 Jaroslav Pelikan, *Luther's Works (Companion Volume): Luther the Expositor* (St. Louis, MO: Concordia, 1959), 54.

40 Ibid. 60, 67 (emphasis added).

41 Brueggemann, *The Book That Breathes New Life*, p. xv.

42 Cosgrove, *Appealing to Scripture in Moral Debate*, ch. 2. It should be noted that Cosgrove's rules are based on what he finds in other hermeneutic writers.

43 Ward, *What the Bible Really Teaches*, 23. It derives from the past participle of the Latin verb *tollere*, "to take away."

44 See e.g. Steve Moyise, *The Old Testament in the New: An Introduction* (New York: Continuum, 2001).

45 Evans, *Is "Holy Scripture" Christian?*, 5; Barton, *People of the Book?*, 4.

46 Ignatius, *Letter to the Philadelphians*, 8. <http://www.ccel.org/ccel/schaff/anf01.v.vi.viii.html>. The passage continues: "To such persons I say that my archives are Jesus Christ, to disobey whom is manifest destruction. My authentic archives are His cross, and death, and resurrection, and the faith which bears on these things, by which I desire, through your prayers, to be justified."

47 Ehrman, *Lost Christianities*, 144.

48 Tertullian, *The Prescription Against Heretics*, tr. P. Holmes, ch. 16. From *The Ante-Nicene Fathers*, vol. III. <http://www.tertullian.org/anf/anf03/anf03-24.htm#P3125_1133921>.

49 Ibid., chs. 17–20.

50 John Leith, "Creeds," in Alan Richardson and John Bowden (eds.), *A New Dictionary of Christian Theology*, 3rd edn. (London: SCM Press, 1985), 131–2: 131.

51 Robert Jenson, "Scripture's Authority in the Church," in Davis and Hays (eds.), *The Art of Reading Scripture*, 27–37: 27.

52 Ibid. 28–9 (emphasis added).

53 Pope Benedict XVI, *Deus Caritas Est* (2005). <http://www.vatican.va/holy_father/benedict_xvi/encyclicals/documents/hf_ben-xvi_enc_20051225_deus-caritas-est_en.html>.

54 Pope Paul VI, *Dogmatic Constitution on Divine Revelation, Dei Verbum* (1965), 1.4. <http://www.vatican.va/archive/hist_councils/ii_vatican_council/documents/vat-ii_const_19651118_dei-verbum_en.html>.

55 Ibid. 2.8, 2.9, 2.10.

56 Ibid. 2.12, 5.18.

57 Ibid. 3.11, 2.10.

Bibliography

Adams, Marilyn McCord, *Christ and Horrors: The Coherence of Christology* (Cambridge: Cambridge University Press, 2006).

American Heritage® Dictionary of the English Language, Fourth Edition. Houghton Mifflin Company, 2004. <http://dictionary.reference.com/browse/type>.

Anderson, Herbert, and Susan B. W. Johnson, *Regarding Children: A New Respect for Childhood and Families* (Louisville, KY: Westminster John Knox Press, 1995).

Bacon, Francis, *The Advancement of Learning*, in *Francis Bacon: The First Book*, ed. W. A. Armstrong (London: Athlone Press, 1975).

Balmer, Randall, *Thy Kingdom Come: How the Religious Right Distorts the Faith and Threatens America (an Evangelical's Lament)* (New York: Basic Books, 2007).

Barth, Karl, *Church Dogmatics*, I.2 (Edinburgh: T&T Clark, 1963).

Barton, John (ed.), *The Cambridge Companion to Biblical Interpretation* (Cambridge: Cambridge University Press, 1998).

Barton, John, *People of the Book? The Authority of the Bible in Christianity*, rev. edn. (London: SPCK, 1993).

Bauckham, Richard J., "Jude," in Bruce M. Metzger and Michael D. Coogan (eds.), *The Oxford Companion to the Bible* (New York and Oxford: Oxford University Press, 1993), 395–7.

Boyer, P., *When Time Shall Be No More: Prophecy Belief in Modern American Culture* (Cambridge, MA: Belknap, 1992).

Brockliss, L., and G. Rousseau (eds.), *Childhood, Violence and the Western Tradition* (Oxford: Oxford University Press, forthcoming).

Brueggemann, Walter, "Biblical Authority in the Postcritical Period," in id., *The Book That Breathes New Life: Scriptural Authority and Biblical Theology* (Minneapolis: Fortress Press, 2005), 3–19.

Bibliography

Brueggemann, Walter, *The Book That Breathes New Life: Scriptural Authority and Biblical Theology* (Minneapolis: Fortress Press, 2005).

Bunge, Marcia J. (ed.), *The Child in Christian Thought* (Grand Rapids, MI: Eerdmans, 2001).

Catechism of the Catholic Church (London: Geoffrey Chapman, 1994).

Coleman, Peter, *Gay Christians: A Moral Dilemma* (London: SCM Press, 1989).

Cone, James H., "Theology's Great Sin: Silence in the Face of White Supremacy," *Black Theology: An International Journal*, 2/2 (July 2004), 139–52.

Congregation for Catholic Education, *Instruction Concerning the Criteria for the Discernment of Vocations with Regard to Persons with Homosexual Tendencies in View of their Admission to the Seminary and to Holy Orders* (2005). <http://www.vatican.va/roman_curia/congregations/ccatheduc/documents/rc_con_ccatheduc_doc_20051104_istruzione_en.html>.

Congregation for the Doctrine of the Faith, *Letter to the Catholic Bishops on the Pastoral Care of Homosexual Persons* (1986). <http://www.vatican.va/roman_curia/congregations/cfaith/documents/rc_con_cfaith_doc_19861001_homosexual-persons_en.html>.

Cooke, Gill, "Christian Forgiveness in Rampton Special Hospital," *Higher Calling* (University of Liverpool Chaplaincy Newsletter).

Cosgrove, Charles H., *Appealing to Scripture in Moral Debate: Five Hermeneutical Rules* (Grand Rapids, MI: Eerdmans, 2002).

Council of Trent (1546), session 4, "Decree concerning the Canonical Scriptures," tr. J. Waterworth (London: Dolman, 1848). <http://history.hanover.edu/texts/trent/ct04.html>.

Crummell, Alexander, *The Future of Africa, being Addresses, Sermons, etc., etc., Delivered in the Republic of Liberia* (New York, 1862).

Crummell, Alexander, "The Negro Race Not under a Curse: An Examination of Genesis IX. 25," in id., *The Future of Africa, being Addresses, Sermons, etc., Delivered in the Republic of Liberia* (New York, 1862).

Curran, Charles E. (ed.), *Change in Official Catholic Moral Teachings* (New York and Mahwah, NJ: Paulist Press, 2003).

d'Costa, Gavin, "Revelation, Scripture and Tradition: Some Comments on John Webster's Conception of 'Holy Scripture'," *International Journal of Systematic Theology*, 6/4 (Oct. 2004), 337–50.

Dalrymple, James, *Institutions of the Laws of Scotland* (1681).

Davies, Philip R. (ed.), *Yours Faithfully: Virtual Letters from the Bible* (London: Equinox, 2004).

Davis, Ellen F., and Richard B. Hays (eds.), *The Art of Reading Scripture* (Grand Rapids, MI: Eerdmans, 2003).

Dawn, Maggi, "Whose Text Is It Anyway? Limit and Freedom in Interpretation," in Duncan Dormor and Jeremy Morris (eds.), *An Acceptable Sacrifice? Homosexuality and the Church* (London: SPCK, 2007), 10–21.

Dehn, G., *Man and Revelation* (London: Hodder & Stoughton, 1936).

Delaney, Carol, *Abraham on Trial: The Social Legacy of Biblical Myth* (Princeton: Princeton University Press, 1998).

Dillen, Annemie, and Didier Pollefeyt (eds.), *Children's Voices: Children's Perspectives in Ethics, Theology, and Religious Education* (Leuven: Peeters, forthcoming).

Dogmatic Constitution on Divine Revelation: Dei Verbum (1965). <http://www.vatican.va/archive/hist_councils/ii_vatican_council/documents/vat-ii_const_19651118_dei-verbum_en.html>.

Dormor, Duncan, and Jeremy Morris (eds.), *An Acceptable Sacrifice? Homosexuality and the Church* (London: SPCK, 2007).

Douglas, Kelly Brown, *What's Faith Go To Do with It? Black Bodies/Christian Souls* (Maryknoll, NY: Orbis Books, 2005).

Ehrman, Bart D., *Lost Christianities: The Battles for Scripture and the Faiths We Never Knew* (New York: Oxford University Press, 2003).

Ehrman, Bart D., *Misquoting Jesus: The Story Behind who Changed the Bible and Why* (New York: HarperSanFrancisco, 2005).

Eiesland, Nancy, *The Disabled God: Towards a Liberation Theology of Disability* (Nashville, TN: Abingdon Press, 1994).

Eusebius, *Church History*. Christian Classics Ethereal Library. <http://www.ccel.org/ccel/schaff/npnf201.iii.viii.v.html>.

Evans, Christopher, *Is "Holy Scripture" Christian? And Other Questions* (London: SCM Press, 1971).

Felder, Cain Hope, "Afrocentrism, the Bible, and the Politics of Difference," *Journal of Religious Thought*, 50/1–2 (Fall 1993/Spring 1994), 45–57.

Felder, Cain Hope (ed.), *Stony the Road We Trod: African American Biblical Interpretation* (Minneapolis: Fortress Press, 1991).

Ford, David, *Christian Wisdom: Desiring God and Learning in Love* (Cambridge: Cambridge University Press, 2007).

Ford, David, and C. C. Pecknold (eds.), *The Promise of Scriptural Reasoning* (Oxford: Blackwell, 2006).

Goldenberg, David M., *The Curse of Ham: Race and Slavery in Early Judaism, Christianity, and Islam* (Princeton, NJ: Princeton University Press, 2003).

Gorringe, Tim, "Political Readings of Scripture," in John Barton (ed.), *The Cambridge Companion to Biblical Interpretation* (Cambridge: Cambridge University Press, 1998), 67–80.

Gribben, Crawford, "Rapture Fictions and the Changing Evangelical Condition," *Literature & Theology*, 18/1 (Mar. 2004), 77–94.

Gundry-Wolf, Judith M., "The Least and the Greatest: Children in the New Testament," in Marcia J. Bunge (ed.), *The Child in Christian Thought* (Grand Rapids, MI: Eerdmans, 2001), 29–60.

Harrison, Peter, *The Bible, Protestantism, and the Rise of Natural Science* (Cambridge: Cambridge University Press, 1998).

Hastings, Adrian, Alistair Mason, and Hugh Pyper (eds.), *The Oxford Companion to Christian Thought* (Oxford: Oxford University Press, 2000).

Hayes, Diana, "Reflections on Slavery," in Charles E. Curran (ed.), *Change in Official Catholic Moral Teachings* (New York and Mahwah, NJ: Paulist Press, 2003), 65–75.

Henson, John, *Good as New: A Radical Retelling of the Scriptures* (New York: O Books, 2004).

Hobbes, Thomas, *Behemoth*, ed. F. Tönnies (London, 1889).

Holder, John, "The Issue of Race: A Search for a Biblical/Theological Perspective," *Journal of Religious Thought*, 49/2 (Winter 1992/Spring 1993), 44–59.

Holloway, Richard, *Godless Morality* (Edinburgh: Canongate, 1999).

Hooker, Richard, *Ecclesiastical Polity Books I–V*, ed. E. Rhys, vol. 1 (London: J. M. Dent, 1907; repr. Everyman's Library, 1925).

Hopkins, John Henry, *A Scriptural, Ecclesiastical, and Historical View of Slavery, from the Days of the Patriarch Abraham, to the Nineteenth Century* (New York: Pooley & Co., 1864).

House of Bishops' Group on Issues in Human Sexuality, *Some Issues in Human Sexuality: A Guide to the Debate* (London: Church House Publishing, 2003).

Ignatius, *Letter to the Philadelphians*. <http://www.ccel.org/ccel/schaff/anf01.v.vi.viii.html>.

Jennings, Theodore W., Jr., *Jacob's Wound: Homoerotic Narrative in the Literature of Ancient Israel* (New York: Continuum, 2005).

Jennings, Theodore W., Jr., *The Man Jesus Loved: Homoerotic Narratives from the New Testament* (Cleveland, OH: Pilgrim Press, 2003).

Jenson, Robert, "Scripture's Authority in the Church," in Ellen F. Davis and Richard B. Hays (eds.), *The Art of Reading Scripture* (Grand Rapids, MI: Eerdmans, 2003), 27–37.

Johnson, William Stacy, "Reading the Scriptures Faithfully in a Postmodern Age," in Ellen F. Davis and Richard B. Hays (eds.), *The Art of Reading Scripture* (Grand Rapids, MI: Eerdmans, 2003), 109–24.

Jordan, Mark D., *The Ethics of Sex* (Oxford: Blackwell, 2002).

Josephus, *War of the Jews* VI.9.3. <http://www.sacred-texts.com/jud/josephus/index.htm>.

Kasper, Walter, "Anti-Semitism: A Wound To Be Healed" (2003). <http://www.vatican.va/roman_curia/pontifical_councils/chrstuni/relations-jews-docs/rc_pc_chrstuni_doc_20030908_kasper-antisemitismo_en.html>.

Katz, David S., *God's Last Words: Reading the English Bible from the Reformation to Fundamentalism* (New Haven: Yale University Press, 2004).

Kierkegaard, Søren, *Fear and Trembling* (1843) (Oxford: Oxford University Press, 1939; Harmondsworth: Penguin Books, 2005).

Knust, Jennifer Wright, *Abandoned to Lust: Sexual Slander and Ancient Christianity* (New York: Columbia University Press, 2006).

Kovacs, Judith, and Christopher Rowland, *Revelation* (Oxford: Blackwell, 2004).

Kramer, Heinrich and James Sprenger, *Malleus Maleficarum* (1948 edn.), tr. Montague Summers (Kessinger Publishing, n.p., n.d.).

Lake, Stephen, *Let the Children Come to Communion* (London: SPCK, 2006).

Lambeth Commission on Communion [The Windsor Report] (London: Church House Publishing, 2004). Online at <http://www.anglicancommunion.org/windsor2004/downloads/windsor2004full.pdf>.

Lambeth Conference 1998, Resolution 1.10c. See <http://www.lambethconference.org/resolutions/1998/1998-1-10.cfm>.

Leith, John, "Creeds," in Alan Richardson and John Bowden (eds.), *A New Dictionary of Christian Theology*, 3rd edn. (London: SCM Press, 1985), 131–2.

Levenson, Jon D., *The Death and Resurrection of the Beloved Son: The Transformation of Child Sacrifice in Judaism and Christianity* (New Haven: Yale University Press, 1993).

Lovering, Eugene H., Jr., and Jerry L. Sumney (eds.), *Theology and Ethics in Paul and His Interpreters* (Nashville: Abingdon Press, 1996).

Lüdemann, Gerd, *The Unholy in Holy Scripture: The Dark Side of the Bible*, tr. John Bowden (London: SCM Press, 1997).

Luther, Martin, *On the Jews and their Lies* (1543). <http://www.humanitas-international.org/showcase/chronography/documents/luther-jews.htm>.

Luther, Martin, *Preface to the Epistles of St. James and St. Jude* (1522).

Luz, Ulrich, *The Theology of the Gospel of Matthew* (Cambridge: Cambridge University Press, 1995).

MacCulloch, Diarmaid, *Reformation: Europe's House Divided 1490–1700* (London: Penguin Books, 2004).

Martin, Dale, *Sex and the Single Saviour* (Louisville, KY: Westminster John Knox Press, 2006).

Martin, David, *Does Christianity Cause War?* (Oxford: Oxford University Press, 1997).

Marvin, Carolyn, and David W. Ingle, *Blood Sacrifice and the Nation: Totem Rituals and the American Flag* (Cambridge: Cambridge University Press, 1999).

Maxwell-Stuart, P. G., *An Abundance of Witches: The Great Scottish Witch-Hunt* (Stroud: Tempus Publishing, 2005).

McGrath, Alister E., *The Christian Theology Reader*, 2nd edn. (Oxford: Blackwell, 2001).

McGrath, Alister E., *Science & Religion: An Introduction* (Oxford: Blackwell, 1999).

Meeks, Wayne A., "The 'Haustafeln' and American Slavery: A Hermeneutical Challenge," in Eugene H. Lovering, Jr., and Jerry L. Sumney (eds.), *Theology and Ethics in Paul and his Interpreters* (Nashville: Abingdon Press, 1996), 232–53.

Mein, Andrew, "Threat and Promise: the Old Testament on Sexuality," in Duncan Dormor and Jeremy Morris (eds.), *An Acceptable Sacrifice? Homosexuality and the Church* (London: SPCK, 2007), 22–32.

Metzger, Bruce M., and Michael D. Coogan (eds.), *The Oxford Companion to the Bible* (New York: Oxford University Press, 1993).

Miller, James E., "The Practices of Romans 1:26: Homosexual or Heterosexual?," *Novum Testamentum*, 37 (1995).

Moore, Gareth, OP, *A Question of Truth: Christianity and Homosexuality* (New York: Continuum, 2003).

Bibliography

Moyise, Steve, *The Old Testament in the New: An Introduction* (New York: Continuum, 2001).

Northcott, Michael, *An Angel Directs the Storm: Apocalyptic Religion & American Empire* (London: I. B. Tauris, 2004).

Oxford English Dictionary, 2nd edn. (1989). <http://dictionary.oed.com/cgi/entry/50195905>.

Pelikan, Jaroslav, *Luther's Works (Companion Volume): Luther the Expositor* (St. Louis, MO: Concordia, 1959).

Pope Benedict XVI, *Deus Caritas Est* (2005). <http://www.vatican.va/holy_father/benedict_xvi/encyclicals/documents/hf_ben-xvi_enc_20051225_deus-caritas-est_en.html>.

Pope Paul VI, *Dogmatic Constitution on Divine Revelation, Dei Verbum* (1965). <http://www.vatican.va/archive/hist_councils/ii_vatican_council/documents/vat-ii_const_19651118_dei-verbum_en.html>.

Pyper, Hugh, "Children," in Adrian Hastings, Alistair Mason, and Hugh Pyper (eds.), *The Oxford Companion to Christian Thought* (Oxford: Oxford University Press, 2000), 110.

Richardson, Alan, and Bowden, John (eds.), *A New Dictionary of Christian Theology*, 3rd edn. (London: SCM Press, 1985).

Rogers, Eugene F., Jr., *Sexuality and the Christian Body* (Oxford: Blackwell, 1999).

Rogerson, John, *Genesis 1–11* (Sheffield: Sheffield Academic Press, 1991).

Ruthven, Malise, *Fundamentalism: The Search for Meaning* (Oxford: Oxford University Press, 2004).

Scroggs, Robin, *The New Testament and Homosexuality* (Philadelphia: Fortress Press, 1983).

Snyder, T. Richard, *The Protestant Ethic and the Spirit of Punishment* (Grand Rapids, MI: Eerdmans, 2001).

Southern Baptist Convention Basic Beliefs: "The Scriptures." <http://www.sbc.net/aboutus/basicbeliefs.asp>.

Southern Baptist Convention Position Statement: "Sexuality." <http://www.sbc.net/aboutus/pssexuality.asp>.

Spong, John Shelby, *The Sins of Scripture* (New York: HarperSanFrancisco: 2005).

Stark, Rodney, *For the Glory of God: How Monotheism Led to Reformations, Science, Witch-Hunts, and the End of Slavery* (Princeton: Princeton University Press, 2003).

Stavrakopoulou, Francesca, *King Manasseh and Child Sacrifice: Biblical Distortions of Historical Realities* (Berlin: Walter de Gruyter, 2004).

Stavrakopoulou, Francesca, "Child Sacrifice in the Ancient World: Blessings for the Beloved," in L. Brockliss and G. Rousseau (eds.), *Childhood, Violence and the Western Tradition* (Oxford: Oxford University Press, forthcoming).

Stuart, Elizabeth, and Adrian Thatcher, *People of Passion: What the Churches Teach about Sex* (London: Mowbray, 1997).

Swartley, Willard M., *Slavery, Sabbath, War & Women* (Scottdale, PA: Herald Press, 1983).

Tertullian, *The Prescription against Heretics*, tr. P. Holmes. From *The Ante-Nicene Fathers*, vol. III. <http://www.tertullian.org/anf/anf03/anf03-24.htm#P3125_1133921>.

Thatcher, Adrian, "Beginning Again with Jesus," in Annemie Dillen and Didier Pollefeyt (eds.), *Children's Voices: Children's Perspectives in Ethics, Theology, and Religious Education* (Leuven: Peeters, forthcoming).

Thatcher, Adrian, *Liberating Sex: A Christian Sexual Theology* (London: SPCK, 1993).

Thatcher, Adrian, *Marriage after Modernity: Christian Marriage in Postmodern Times* (Sheffield and New York: Sheffield Academic Press/New York University Press, 1999).

Thatcher, Adrian, "Some Issues with 'Some Issues in Human Sexuality,'" *Theology and Sexuality*, 11/3 (May, 2005), 9–30.

Thatcher, Adrian, *Theology and Families* (Oxford: Blackwell, 2007).

Thatcher, Adrian, *Truly a Person, Truly God* (London: SPCK, 1990).

von Rad, Gerhard, *Genesis* (London: SCM Press, 1961).

Wallis, Jim, *God's Politics: Why the Right Gets It Wrong and the Left Doesn't Get It* (Oxford: Lion Publishing, 2006).

Ward, Keith, *What the Bible Really Teaches: A Challenge for Fundamentalists* (London: SPCK, 2004).

Webster, John, *Holy Scripture: A Dogmatic Sketch* (Cambridge: Cambridge University Press, 2003).

Weems, Renita J., "Reading *Her Way* through the Struggle: African American Women and the Bible," in Cain Hope Felder (ed.), *Stony the Road We Trod: African American Biblical Interpretation* (Minneapolis: Fortress Press, 1991), 57–80.

Wimbush, Vincent L., "The Bible and African Americans: An Outline of an Interpretative History," in Cain Hope Felder (ed.), *Stony the Road We*

Bibliography

Trod: African American Biblical Interpretation (Minneapolis: Fortress Press, 1991), 81–97.

Windsor Report, see *Lambeth Commission on Communion.*

Wittgenstein, Ludwig, *Philosophical Investigations*, tr. G. E. M. Anscombe (Oxford: Blackwell, 1972).

Working Party Commissioned by the House of Bishops of the Church of England, *Marriage in Church After Divorce* (London: Church House Publishing, 2000).

Index of Scriptural Citations

General Index